SPIRIT
MEDICINE

Donna McGee

SPIRIT
MEDICINE

Native American Teachings to Awaken the Spirit

WOLF MOONDANCE

Illustrated by Jim Sharpe & Sky Starhawk

STERLING PUBLISHING CO., INC.   NEW YORK

By the same author
RAINBOW MEDICINE

Library of Congress Cataloging-in-Publication Data

Moondance, Wolf.
    Spirit medicine : Native American teachings to awaken the spirit /
Wolf Moondance ; illustrated by Jim Sharpe and Sky Starhawk.
        p.   cm.
    Includes index.
    ISBN 0-8069-1368-1
    1. Medicine wheels—Miscellanea.   2. Spiritual life.   I. Title.
BF1623.M43M66   1995
299'.75—dc20   95-20796
                                                           CIP
                                                           REV.

10 9 8 7 6 5 4 3 2

Published by Sterling Publishing Company, Inc.
387 Park Avenue South, New York, N.Y. 10016
© 1995 by Wolf Moondance
Additional illustrations © 1995 by Jim Sharpe
Distributed in Canada by Sterling Publishing
% Canadian Manda Group, One Atlantic Avenue, Suite 105
Toronto, Ontario, Canada M6K 3E7
Distributed in Great Britain and Europe by Cassell PLC
Wellington House, 125 Strand, London WC2R 0BB, England
Distributed in Australia by Capricorn Link (Australia) Pty Ltd.
P.O. Box 6651, Baulkham Hills, Business Centre, NSW 2153, Australia
Manufactured in the United States of America
All rights reserved

Sterling ISBN 0-8069-1368-1

Donna McKee

Contents

To sunshine, to moonbeams, to scattering stars.
To dragons and butterflies.
To today, tomorrow, and forever.

This book is dedicated to Granny Lil for her chocolate cake. It is dedicated to my father-in-law for being a decent man, and to my mom for being Native American. It is dedicated to my sister, Betty, who continues to follow. It is dedicated to my nephews, Tyler and Josh, and my niece, Oddie, who are the next generation. It is dedicated to Raven, all my love.

Purpose

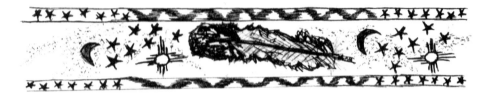

The purpose of Spirit Medicine is to open a door to the quest for the spirit self. Spirit Medicine is a teaching from Rainbow Medicine. Rainbow Medicine is teachings from the Rainbow Medicine Wheel, which comes from the vision of the sun, moon, and seven stars that was given to me, Wolf Moondance.

I am Osage, Cherokee, and English, born and raised in Oklahoma. I walk the medicine way. I live in two worlds—Native and white. When I walk in the Native world, I'm white. And when I walk in the white world, I'm Native. There came a time in my life when I didn't know where to walk, so I walked my vision. It brought me through Rainbow Medicine, through listening to the stars, to a place known as the Quest for the Whole Self. In this classroom setting people achieve mental medicine; they achieve emotional medicine; they achieve physical medicine; they receive Spirit Medicine.

Within Spirit Medicine we walk the teachings of memory and listen for the voice of the spirit. We build bundles, honor our tools, learn how to have visions. Since I received my vision as a child, in the form of the sun, the moon, and the seven stars, it has guided every moment of my life, for I am dedicated and committed to visioning. I am a visionary, a way of Wisdom—one who teaches the Way—the wolf. Spirit Medicine is my vision. My vision is the Rainbow Medicine Wheel. My teachings are Rainbow Medicine. They bring forth answers to lessons. They make lessons into teachings. They set us in a solid way. I live in old ways. I walk within the lodge. I teach in a tepee. I teach by the river. I teach with the dirt. I teach with the air. I teach with the fire.

Spirit Medicine is a work for you to bring forth your spirit—to have a medicine wheel and understand that everyone is welcome there, but the ways are strict, the disciplines are hard, and the commitment is deep. In physical presence, it will take one year to complete the lessons and apply the medicines in this book. About the time you get to the bottom, you are just beginning to fly. But within Spirit Medicine there is no time. Within spirit there is no time. There is no racism. There is no judgment.

There is evil. There is bad. There is good. There is heavenly. All that spirit is, comes from the heart of the eagle. These are the ways of Spirit Medicine.

As you read this book, you will be in a school within spirit, a mystery school. You will explore beliefs that will better your life and beliefs that will open up to your spirit. You will feel the medicine of the river that is the heart of our lodge. You will connect to the spirit world and hear teachers from the upper world. Open your heart and allow your mind, body, and emotions to listen to your spirit. Walk within the stars and heal the scars. Understand that your walk must be the same as your talk. Spirit Medicine will give you the ability to treat the broken wing, the broken heart, the broken mind, the broken spirit, and stand firmly on the medicine. You will share the heart of the elk, walk with the cat, feel the life of the buffalo. You will spiral in the soft circle of the hawk, sense the deep feelings of the sleeping bear, walk with pride at the flight of the eagle. And you will hear the call of the wolf. I invite you to the spirit mystery school.

Aho.

Prelude

I was invited by Grandfather Snake one time to be part of the brotherhood and sisterhood of transformation. I was given the vision of the sun, the moon, and the seven stars to enable us to grow and find our direction through study. I was shown the medicine wheel, which has been used by the wise teachers, mothers and fathers, aunties and uncles, grandmothers and grandfathers, to teach by laying out stones that have meaning—or sticks—or bones—or rocks. Lessons are connected to these objects. My teachings are contemporary, so while you are laying out the stones in old ways, you will also be using them in new ways.

At a medicine wheel there are gateways that you step through. The gateways represent the reality between the physical and the spiritual. In Spirit Medicine you will travel in the spirit section of the medicine wheel. You will be working only in the East, working on spiritual lessons. You will be learning, finding and dealing with the spirit part of yourself. Each lesson, each teaching, each medicine, is to be applied with the understanding that it speaks to your spirit. Your spirit has a totem guide, and that is an eagle. So while you are working on the processes in this part of the medicine wheel, be at peace in mind and heart with the great eagle. When you hear it or see it, you'll know you are in communication with Great Spirit, for your spirit is a point of Great Spirit.

It is my hope, my dream, and my vision that Spirit Medicine will open a door to transformation and to a wholeness that will allow you to dance within your sacred self.

Aho.

· 1 ·
THE BEAUTY OF
THE BLUE SKY

Before me I see the sun, the crescent moon, and seven stars. I breathe in and out, relax and let go. I continue breathing, and with each breath I give honor. For many years have passed since I was five years of age. I have listened to spirit voices throughout my life. The voices of the stars have carried me into now, where I stand with my vision as an adult. It is mine, I know, to walk the way of the sun and the moon and seven stars. It is something I hold dear inside my heart, for I have listened to the voice of the stars many times. My ways in life are not the same as others. For I listen to spirit.

Tonight I sit alone in the mountains, watching the moon, watching the beauty of blue in the sky. I hear the call of the wolf. Before me I see a familiar path. This path is filled with pastel color. I see the soft purple calling me. I hear the wolf howling through the mountains and the night sky. The colors become more intense. I find myself walking the familiar path through the mountains. It carries me past the gnarled trees that open the door to the spirit world. I come upon a camp where the light is many colors. It is soft peach; it is soft yellow; it is lime green—pale and minty. It is soft pale blue. These colors are cool. Morning stars twinkle around us.

Before me I see a council of spirits sitting around a fire. There is a blue one—rich, transparent blue. The spirit is that of a fire spirit, yet it sits alone, near the fire but separate from it. Beside it is the spirit of red—transparent red—shimmery but solid. This spirit has long, flame-looking fingers. Next to it is a yellow spirit, a clear and clean, soft yellow. Its features are that of a flame, yet it too is outside the circle of fire, sitting on the ground in council. Next to it is a green spirit, haggard and deep, but soft. Beveled and pointed, it sits hunched with arms crossed and knees bent. Next to it is the spirit of purple. It is dark; it is light; it is foreboding and inviting. It is jagged, pointed, and ruffled. It sits there brooding, yet soft and inviting. Next to it is the orange spirit. Its head is pointed, as are its feet. It too is flame-like, yet is an entity of its own. Within its orange softness, I can see other colors cycling and swirling. Next to it sits the burgundy spirit. It is stoic, majestic, rich, and transparent.

I look closer at the spirits, and they all have stars for eyes. Their bodies are stars—no, they're flames—no, stars. Well, they're flame-like star spirits. That's a good way to say it. They are all sitting in council, waiting for something.

The wind blows softly. I feel a presence behind me. I hear the wind call my name, "Wolf." I listen quietly. I hear, "Very carefully." Grandmother Wolf says, "Very carefully, sit with the spirits, and remember. Sit within the spirit band you are from. Sit quietly. And remember."

I move towards the blue band, the soft blue spirit. I am drawn to the blue and feel that I should sit with it. I sit quietly and listen to the wind blow through the spirits. The wind blows through me. Emerging in the center of the fire is a majestic, grand white star, rising in the smoke from the fire. This white star is so white it is blue, and so blue it's white. It is a very powerful presence. This star resonates above us, and as it does, the spirits and I begin to swirl. We spin around the fire and become one with it. We rise and go through the star. As we enter the white star, there is a brightness—a completeness of bright white light.

"Remember. Remember," I hear the voice of Grandfather Wolf.

"What do you see, Wolf?"

I see the white star evolving. I see a mist of color, spiralling up as fog rises above the white star. It's like smoke coming out of a bowl of dry ice, filtering down over the edges of the star. The smoke is swirling color—rich red, rich orange, rich green, rich yellow, rich blue, rich purple, rich burgundy. These colors spin out, floating down over the star. I feel myself sliding down the blue band of smoke, and then I am standing in the beautiful countryside.

The greens are bright; the grass is green. The blue is bright; the sky is blue. The clouds are bright; the clouds are all colors—soft pale yellow, pale pinks, and bright purples, bright yellow—color everywhere.

I see spirits running to and fro, the same spirits who sat by the fire, only different colors—paler colors, darker ones, brighter colors, softer ones. I take time to look at these spirits, and I see that all of them have levels, depths within them. As I concentrate on one spirit, I see that it is a flower, for I see a white rose. It is a plant, for I see a cottonwood within it. It is a rock, for I see granite. It is an animal, for I see a wolf. It is a person, for I see myself. I look at the spirit that is reflected back in the pond that I peer into. There are different levels of this spirit: a human, an animal, a tree, a rock, a flower. And I see its spirit form, the color. It is blue with tints of burgundy. Then I see a star, pointed on the edges— a star shape. This spirit is all, it is ancient.

"Yes, Granddaughter. It is ancient. It is everything within the clan it walks with. It is you."

I turn and there stands Grandmother Wolf, twinkling burgundy stars in her eyes. Grandfather Wolf is standing behind her with his paws on her shoulders. These are old wolf spirits! She shimmers of crystal. He shimmers of opal.

"Your rocks are different from mine."

"Yes. Every rock within a personality will be different. For every personality is an individual, unique to its own levels of self. One might be one flower and be of the same blue and be of a different clan, yellow."

"Grandmother, Grandfather. There are ancient truths here in this place."

"You are home, Granddaughter. This is your home."

The wind rushes past us and the leaves tumble. I hear joyful laughter as they roll past me. "Leaf spirits."

"Yes, singing leaf spirits," Grandmother smiles. "Everything here is a spirit."

"This place is spirit" Grandfather replies. "It is all spirit—the color, the physicality. For you are in the physical stage of spirit. Sit down, Granddaughter, and we will teach you of this spirit."

As I sit, I am joined by a like spirit. I turn my head. The spirit turns its head. I turn my head the other way; it turns its head the other way.

"Who are you?"

The spirit looks at me and smiles. "I am your brother spirit. You are my sister spirit. You are my brother spirit, I am your sister spirit. You and I are whole."

Grandmother looks at me and says, "It is within these two spirits that the Good Road and the Spirit Road live."

I turn my head, and there are two more spirits. They turn their heads. My brother spirit and I turn our heads. They turn their heads.

"You are brother/sister spirit. We are your brother/sister spirit."

The four of us take hands and we circle around Grandmother/Grandfather Wolf's spirit. We dance around the spirit. Grandmother/Grandfather Wolf become a white star of crystal and opal—a beautiful burgundy rose and a white daisy—two cottonwoods. Around them the river flows. A powerful spirit, this circle of four!

We sit and listen to Grandmother/Grandfather Spirit tell us the ways of the old world, the ways of home, the center, the core, the vibrating force. "Here within this place, all is spirit and good. From you are the Blue Roads and Red Roads. For you are gates, the North, South, East, and West. As you spiral around, you encompass life. You *are* life as it pours out of us. As we walk, we extend the path. We are the path. Then from the four of us, it is six, and then seven. And then eight, and then nine. Nine angels I see," Grandmother smiles. "A silver one and a gold one have joined you, a rainbow of spirits with silver and gold now entwine, making a rope, spiraling around and around. Now they are seven with one above, a silver sky, and one below, a golden ground.

"From this rainbow of color and silver and gold, sparks fly out, lightning flashes, thunder rolls. Color sparks and spits and spirals and spurts. Sparks of light fly everywhere. Stars shimmer and twinkle, bouncing, scattering stars everywhere. Sets of children, tiny stars dancing."

"All is," Grandfather says. "All is."

The animals sing. The day is bright and clear. More sparks of light and family emerges—spirit family. All. Clusters of color. Band of blue. Grandmother/Grandfather Wolf. Band of red. Band of orange. Band of yellow. Band of green. Band of purple. Band of burgundy. The band is the whole color that every spirit is a point of. All seven bands are full and rich points of light. As far as one can see, color is everywhere.

I remember Grandmother/Grandfather Wolf. I remember my home— the tulips and jonquil, daffodils and gladiolas. All color. I remember pear and peach trees—the flowering, flaming maple. All color. I remember the magnolia, the mums, the shrubs and hedges, the green grass, the hillside, the grapes. All color. I remember tomatoes and potatoes. I remember carrots. I remember all, a vibrating resonant color.

"It is important to remember the order. Look in the sky, Granddaughter. Look at the order. And remember. Remember, Granddaughter. Remember. Remember the order."

I look at the sky, and there is the sun. I see red and orange and yellow. I look at the sky in the other direction and I see the crescent moon, blue, green, purple, and burgundy. The sky is a soft pink and blue, a perfect mesh of both colors. In the sky I see stars, seven.

"Well, Grandmother, I remember. I see my vision. I've walked within the direction of the sun, and I know the gates of the North, the South, the East, and the West. I've listened to the medicines of the moon, the teachings of women. I know these teachings. And the star voices are Rainbow Medicine."

The stars become one, forming a path of red, orange, yellow, green, blue, purple, and burgundy.

"This path is a road that you must walk. It has been shown to you, Granddaughter, that you follow this path, for you are Wolf. You are from the blue band. You walk within the burgundy clan. You are from the teacher's teachers. You are the one who walks with the knowledge. You are the one who walks with the teachings of the stars. Take this pouch."

The pouch she hands me is burgundy, and off the side of it trail silver stars. At the bottom are seven stars—red, orange, yellow, green, blue, purple, and burgundy.

"Take this, Granddaughter." She holds out a black hat. "You will remember your pain. Your pain will become what it is. Peace. Acceptance. Intelligence. And now."

I hold the black hat. I am standing in now. Now—a place that is real in the physical realm, where I am a human two-legged and walk with the spirit of the White Wolf. I have chosen to follow the spiritual life, to live the way of a shaman, to give my heart to individualism, to follow the ways of spirit. I look inside this hat, and there I see a burgundy bag with silver stars, with a red one, an orange one, a yellow one, a green one, a blue one, a purple one, and a burgundy one. The spirit of this bag is strong. As I look into the hat, I remember my father, who owned it, who wore it as a bull rider. He walked in an intense way and brought abuse to everything he touched. I took a deep breath, and, as I did, the bag came untied. My hat was full of stars. They spilled out over the edges. They became a path in front of me.

"Follow the path, Granddaughter. Teach. Teach the Spirit Medicine that you know. Call classes together. Write. Share your words with others. Walk the sacred Rainbow Path. Respect the ways of all people. Stop abuse. Teach. Teach Spirit Medicine, for it is the time for the star people to speak."

In front of me I see a park-like setting—green grass. It is springtime. A river rushes by. I see the medicine wheel, the poles, the colored flags. Rocks. I see an ancient medicine setting.

"This is a place of teaching, Granddaughter. It is a place we have brought you to listen to the snake. It is yours now, to listen to the vision of the bear. Hear his personal medicine wheel. Recall your own medicine wheel. Teach from the Mother Wheel, the Rainbow Medicine Wheel. Come here and look."

I walk within the gates of the medicine wheel—it is someone else's, someone else's program. People dance and sing. People cry and laugh. We sway together as the Rainbow energy moves us. Energy entwines in each of us, calling our memory forth. Mine is awakened.

The path goes on and I follow it.

"Bring forth your vision, Granddaughter," Grandfather Wolf says. "Listen to Grandfather/Grandmother Spirit. Pray your prayer, your prayer of vision, and listen."

I went out by the river and prayed my prayer. "Aho, Grandmother/ Grandfather Spirit. Fill my heart with truth. Show me the Impeccable Way. Let me teach the words of Spirit Medicine. Let me show the way to remember and to hold within us the sacred truths of the Spirit Path. Let me walk within the Mother Wheel, the Rainbow Medicine Wheel. Let me see the Rainbow Medicines and teach the lessons. Let me share with those whose hearts are thirsty for spirit. Open the way and let me teach Spirit Medicine—the section of the wheel that is in the East—the Medicine of Great Spirit, Grandmother/Grandfather, represented by the eagle. Show me now the ways of Spirit Medicine."

I hear the soft sound of the flute calling me back.

Spirit Journal

Tools: *A notebook of a color that represents your spirit; paper; pen; glue; glitter; beads; leather; construction paper; gift wrapping paper; 100 percent cotton cloth in seven colors (red, orange, yellow, green, blue, purple, burgundy); glue gun; scissors; sequins; sage or sweet grass. Be sure that red is also connected to the notebook for the spirit teachings are of the East, and red is the color of East.*

A spirit journal is a notebook for you to keep during the teachings of Spirit Medicine so that you have a daily record of your feelings that are spiritual. It is also a place where you can record your dreams, see the spiritual parts of your dreams, and write them down. The spiritual parts of your dreams would be the lessons you receive—the place in your dream where someone comes and teaches you something, or where some part of your dream explains something to you.

You need to write in your spirit journal daily, and to review it during the week and the month, so that you can absorb the full meaning of the teachings.

Smudging

Putting a small amount of sage or sweet grass in a bowl, light it with a match and quickly blow out the flame. Smoke will rise softly. Pass all the objects you are going to use, including your notebook, through the smoke four times, to remove negative energy. This is called "smudging."

When you work on a spirit notebook, you are building a spirit journal. The notebook part of the journal can be a three-ring binder or two pieces of cardboard or wood that you have drilled holes through so you can tie them together with sinew, yarn, or heavy string. The spirit part of the journal is the creativity that goes into the project. I have listed ideas in the "Tools" section for you to work from. You may want to use pages of different colors, because they will mean different things to you, as the colors mean different things.

You can personalize the outside of your journal to make it yours. Wrap it with skin, paper, or cloth. Use sequins, sew on cloth, bead it, glitter it, glue it. Put pictures on it. You can do anything you want to cover your notebook and make a journal, a home for your sacred writings—writings of the spirit. In this place you will keep your memories, your dreams, your conversations with the spirit world, with guides, with angels, with Christ, with Great Spirit, with grandmothers and grandfathers and ones who have walked into the East, the ancestor realm. It is a place where colors will speak to you. The symbols that are on your spirit journal reflect what you are and who you are.

Because it is important to be able to communicate with spirit, it is important to keep notes—because the spirits see. They look down from the upper world onto Earth Mother. When they speak to us, they can be right on our shoulder. Those that are on our shoulder are guardian angels or spirits.

You'll want to make a spirit entry every day—sometimes four times, sometimes seven times, sometimes only once. To keep it sacred, do it one or four or seven times, because these are sacred numbers. It's important to record the date and the time, and it is a good thing to write down the place you're in and a little bit about what is going on around you. A spirit journal is for communicating with your inner self—past imagination—in the spirit world. Here you can listen and make sense of what you hear.

Remember when you are working in a spirit journal not to write only half sentences, or just bits and pieces of what you see, because these are only flashes of spirit memory. You want to have a full paragraph or a full text, not just scraps, because you'll need to make sense of what is being said to you. Confusion distorts, twists, withers, decays, and destroys. Clean, clear understanding allows you to grow and expand. When you are working in your spirit journal, you are making sense of what you are seeing in your daily life. A spirit journal will keep your clear thoughts in order.

To walk with clarity from your spirit, you need to be able to interpret the animal world, the rock world, the plant world, the colors. You need to bring them forth through your interpretation. There are many places and many teachers who have their own interpretations. There is no right or wrong, and all words have many possible meanings. Take your writings to their depths, bring them into wholeness for you—and put them to work in your world. Making the spirit journal yours is a process of owning your medicine.

Within Spirit Medicine, the keeping of a spirit journal is essential. Writing our entries daily is important. A major feature of your writing is to make a list every night that is known as "1–25." In it, you list the things that you are going to do the next day. During the day, look at the list. Do the things that need to be done, and when you have finished each one, check it off. If you do not finish any item, circle it and move it to the next day's list. This is important, because it keeps your day organized.

When you are not using your spirit journal, keep it in a special travelling case, or wrap it in red cotton cloth and place it inside another object, such as a medicine bag or purse that you carry with you. Your respect for your spirit journal is very important. It teaches you respect for the self.

Spirit Medicine Bundle

Tools: *Sage or sweet grass; 100 percent cotton cloth that represents the color of your spirit; objects that are considered spiritual (pine cones to represent growing, rocks to represent security and solidness, things that you bring forth that are part of your spirit bundle).*

A spirit bundle is made by achieving a connection with your spirit, by understanding the spirit medicines and bringing forth a symbol that connects to each of them. Spirit Medicine within these teachings are Confidence, Balance, Creativity, Growth, Truth, Wisdom, and Impeccability. These are spiritual medicine—word medicine, words that treat the spirit. With Confidence they treat spirit; with Balance they treat self-love; with Creativity they treat movement; with Growth they treat innocence; with Truth they treat loyalty; with Wisdom they treat prayer; and with Impeccability they treat worth.

The spirit bundle will reinforce your connection with your spirit. To bring forth the knowledge of your spirit is to bring out your inner self.

Spirit Medicine Bundle

There are many different times when you might feel it necessary to have a spirit bundle: when you want to lift your spirits and clear away sadness; when you are in the process of studying your spirit; when you feel the need to honor the spirit; when you understand and know the spirit better through symbols; when you need to converse with the spirit through symbols; for a naming; when, in the process of sharing during a marriage, you want the other one to see your spirit; or when you are in the process of preparing to drop your robe, which is to die a physical death. Spirit bundles bring you joy, set your spirit in Confidence (which is Spirit Medicine), and help you learn the lesson of Patience.

Building your spirit bundle is an empowering process. You keep your bundle inside a cloth that is the color of your spirit. To know the color of your cloth, sit in silence with your spirit and you'll see a color; you'll hear a color; you'll smell a color; you'll think a color; you'll know a color. That color is the color of your spirit. This is the color of the bundle that you build. Just as the color of your spirit can change due to the growth of your spirit, so too your bundle can change colors on the outside, whenever you sense that your spirit has changed. The color you come up with for your spirit is the color that your spirit is asking for, the one it needs to be treated with.

Example: *If you see green, then you need to treat your spirit with growth; you need to let your spirit come out, to expand, for it needs to bring forth its innocence.*

In the bundle you'll place things that are of your spirit. You will do this by walking your daily life and connecting with things that feel comfortable. For instance, let's say that a red rose is very comfortable and feels very familiar—then, place a red rose in your bundle. Or say you go to the ocean and walk along the shore. It may feel very comfortable to pick up ocean shells and rocks—place these in your bundle. These things bring you a feeling of connectedness, of knowing that you are a part of something larger, that your spirit is speaking to you. Or you may walk among the pines, in the woods, and an oak tree may speak to you by giving you an acorn, or a pine may speak to you by giving you a cone or pine needles. If you feel that these things are a part of your spirit, put them in your spirit bundle. It is good, when you take something from the earth, to leave a giveaway—such as sweet grass, sage, tobacco, or cornmeal. If you don't have anything else with you, leave a hair or spit.

When you connect with your spirit in the Ceremony of Memory, you will find more spirit connections: the type of rock, the type of tree, the type of flower, the type of animal. All these things, or representations of them, are to go in your spirit bundle.

A spirit bundle is to be used in memory of the self, of the spirit self. You can place it in the center of our medicine wheel. You can keep it in your home in a sacred place. We call that an altar. Keep the bundle fresh and alive by putting sweet grass and fresh sage inside it. The full moon is the time to freshen or add new herbs to your bundle.

When you open your bundle, always burn sweet grass or sage. Put the bundle through the smoke four times to honor what is inside.

You may feel you want to close your bundle at times when you need

Setting Up an Altar

To set up a personal altar, place a 100 percent cotton cloth on a table or on the floor. On it you can place sacred objects, such as your spirit bundle. Always use votive candles on your altar and put them on clay saucers, the kind you see at greenhouses or floral supply houses. Soak the saucer for up to 30 minutes before setting the candle on it. This kind of holder is better than a glass one, because glass may shatter from the heat, but clay won't as long as it's moist.

Keep on your altar: a white candle, to represent Great Spirit; a small bowl of water to represent cleansing—at the full moon, spill the water out onto the earth and refill the bowl; a bowl of cornmeal to feed the Earth; a saucer of fresh dirt to honor the Earth.

to close down your spirit. That may be at a time when you go into grief, or into a place that is separated from the light, or when you are in the process of making life changes. You would then close your bundle and pack it away in a safe place. You would reopen the bundle when you are ready to listen and honor your spirit.

When times are good, a spirit bundle should be open to let your spirit sing. When your spirit bundle is open, you will have a good feeling, remembering that your spirit comes first in the Medicine Wheel. Then say a prayer and close the bundle by placing first the right corner over the center (which represents the East), next the left corner over the center, and then pull the bottom corner up over the center and roll it towards the top. Tie it with a string.

There may be times when you want to break your bundle down and no longer use a spirit bundle. You might want to do this to give thanks to your spirit for showing you the symbols in the bundle, or to clear any negativity from your life. To break down the bundle, open it, take the things out and put them back where they came from. The pine cones, for example, would go back under the tree, the shells back to the shore. When you do this, you turn the symbols of your spirit free, disrobing the spirit bundle. Finish by keeping only a piece of cloth that represents your color. That cloth is to be folded and put away until you feel it is necessary to make a spirit bundle again.

· 2 ·

SUN, MOON, AND SEVEN STARS
The Call of the Wolf

I breathe in and out and relax. A calmness comes over me. I continue breathing. When I feel empty, I'm afraid, alone, and scared. I want to keep breathing, but the air feels like it's cut off and I can't. I take a deep breath and let it out. I wait, but I do not see anything. An emptiness is all I hear, all I feel. How do I find the path?

Maybe the path is the stars. I'll think of them. There's a red one, and an orange one, a yellow one, a green one, a blue one, a purple one, and a burgundy one. The star path turns into a rainbow path and then becomes seven stars. They darken and soon disappear.

I relax and lean back into the comfort of the ground. I hear a fire crackling and popping. I feel cool air around me. I lie very still on the ground, wrapped in my medicine blanket.

It's time—the time of the sun and the moon and the seven stars. I know the vision. I've walked with the teachings of Grandmother Wolf, and I'm ready to teach. I'm eager. I'll get up off this ground in the real world. I'm old enough; I'm strong enough; I'm not alone. I look deep into my mind, beyond imagination, into the realm of journey. My spirit eyes long to see and there is darkness.

Then a piercing howl, a call of the wolf. I hear this low, moaning sound piercing the night, piercing the darkness in my vision. Standing in the spirit world I'm confronted with a mirror. In the mirror I see me. Wolf. Woman. The mirror is very clear, very peaceful. My reflection waves. I wave back. What a funny feeling! You're waving at me, and I'm me. I should be waving at you while you wave back!

"No. Not here," my reflection replies. "Here, I can wave at you and you'll wave at me. You'll wave at me and I'll wave at you. Because I'm real and you're real."

"But, you're me," I reply.

"No, I'm your reflection."

And from the mirror my reflection steps out with me. Finally, I'm in the spirit world! I didn't think I'd ever get here again. Each time I go to journey, I wonder if there will be anything.

My reflection starts to walk ahead of me. "There is always a spirit world, and there is always a place for you in the upper world. There is always someone to teach you."

My reflection and I walk to a place of cool green grass. There are two rocks, the perfect size to sit on. My reflection extends her paw hand and says, "Join me." She sits on the rock with her beautiful tail curled around her legs. I sit on the rock.

"Do I look like you?"

"You look like me. I look like you," my reflection says. "We're the same. Wolf. Woman. We're the same. I'm your reflection and you're me."

"Hmmm. I always wondered what it would be like to look at me. I never thought about seeing both the spirit and the physical. It's very hard, you know, when you look in the mirror on Earth and see a human. You see a two-legged and don't see the spirit part of yourself. It's very hard."

My reflection kind of smiles in her eyes. The side of her that I can see is wolf. The other side is me, my familiar, two-legged, human face.

"I am your guide. Your reflection holds within it the story of your spirit and your physicality. The wolf is your animal totem to your spirit. You know this. You are this. For you have been born to teach the ways—medicine ways, ways of lessons, ways of teachings. You have transitional tools to give the two-legged, ways to change their lives, to call upon the stars and heal their scars. This is your calling."

"Is everyone called by the wolf?" I ask my reflection.

"No. Wolves are called by the wolf. The ways of learning call all people. There are many teachers who hold within their heart wolf medicine. It is not unusual to see a horse teach. It is not unusual to see a mountain lion teach. It is not unusual to see a raven or an eagle teach or to listen to the lessons of the bear. Here within the spirit world, here where the teachings of Spirit Medicine live, it's not unusual to see anyone preparing a lecture to take back and gift the two-legged to make them more comfortable on their earthly walk."

"Oh, the earthly walk. You know, Reflection, I haven't figured that out."

"Shh."

A swirling wind is beginning to build. Leaves blow all around me. The wind howls and spins and I can hear breaking glass, fracturing sounds. I hear sounds of rocks sliding, pushing, tearing through the earth, a crushing of bones, a cracking of stone. I feel the wind blow hard against me. I find myself lying beside a pond. I look up and nothing is familiar. Of course, there is no rock and no reflection.

"Remember. I'm always here, inside you. You are me and I am you."

Oh, my head hurts. Those sounds! The wind! I look at the sky, and there is the sun—full, strong, and powerful. On the other side of me is a crescent moon, and up above me, in a circle spiralling down towards me, seven stars. The colors around me are different. They are not ordinary—not the colors I see on Earth Mother. They are all soft shades. There is purple, and there is lavender. There is blue, and there is sky blue. There is green, and there is pale mint green. There is orange, and there is a soft peach color. There is red and pink. There is very deep yellow and very soft yellow. There is burgundy and soft mauve. The colors are everything. There are mauve trees, and there are green bushes. The water is pale, pale pastel blue and pink, soft orange and dark, rich blue, and dark, rich green. The fused light is soft around me.

This place. . . . Oh, my head. Oh, yes . . . am I in the spirit world? I must be. I recognize the rich colors. I hear a galloping horse go past me. I see a black horse pass. Up ahead of me, a woman walks. I recognize this person.

"Wait a minute! Wait a minute! Let me catch up with you!"

I jump to my feet and hurry towards her. Rapidly I approach the woman. I go through her — run right through her! I stop and turn, looking back. There is a wise one standing there.

"May I help you?"

"Yes — the woman that I was running towards — the young woman with the long hair. Excuse me, I thought you were her."

"There is no one here but me."

"But you have long silver hair, and you're an elder." Before me is a willowy, tall old woman with long glistening hair pulled back in a braid. She wears a cape of many colors, trimmed in silver bells. Her boots are made of coyote, her gloves of mink and mouse, and the little paws wave at me. Her clothes seem to be made out of grass; her shirt spun of many different grasses. Her skirt is different kinds of sticks — small, woven together. Her belt is tied with seashells and small pieces of driftwood, moss, and seaweed. Her eyes are deep and dark. In her right eye, I see the sun, in her left eye, the moon. Around her neck hang seven stars.

"I'm Grandmother Vision. Can I help you?"

"Yes. I'm Wolf."

"I know. You've been called. To me — your Vision. Let's walk and we'll talk."

We begin to walk through this place. The surroundings are familiar, yet strange—mountains, a river, large cottonwood trees and the wind blows through them. The river is full of fish. It is autumn, and the fresh smell is around me. Ahead of me I see a camp. Some red cloth tied on a stick blows in the breeze. Small smoke circles spiral above a fire. I see a grass hut—at least, it looks like grass. As we come closer, I see it is made of sticks and grass and rosebushes that are all in bloom. It is a beautiful hut, with red roses and yellow ones, orange roses and blue ones, purple roses and deep, rich burgundy ones. Green is in their leaves. The hut is a rainbow rose hut.

It is quiet in the camp. A black and white spotted horse grazes in the grass.

"Join me for dinner and we'll talk."

I sit with Grandmother Vision. She tells me that I am in the upper world, that I have come to her for teachings.

"Each person on the Earth Mother comes to me, and asks me for their vision, and I look at them with their vision. They see it, you see it, in me."

"Yes, Grandmother. I see it. I see the moon and the sun and the seven stars. I've had that vision since I was a child."

"You are that vision," she says. "And while you're on the Earth, you walk with the call of the wolf. You have been called to teach. You have been called to walk—as a student, as a teacher, as a master of teaching, as a grandmaster of teaching, as a grand teacher. As a shaman. You will teach eternally. Those who call, you will answer. This is the way of the wolf."

I feel a humbleness—it makes me feel as if I've aged. My head drops. "Grandmother Vision, it is me, to teach always, for I am Blue. I am of the blue band and I walk with the burgundy clan." I look her in the eye and she smiles.

"Here in the upper world you will meet other teachers who will share with you the lessons needed to help the two-legged find their sacred self. It is important that humans remember their spirit. It is important that humans walk a fleshly walk, a walk of death and decay, of disappointment and anguish, of trials and tribulations, of abandonment and separation. Times get hard for humans," says Grandmother.

A sadness moves toward me, but as it starts to enter me, a warm, rich feeling comes and the sadness spirals around me instead. I feel the presence of my reflection and remember that I am wolf. I feel the strength of the wolf, and I move quickly away from the sadness. It puts me to the other side of Grandmother Vision. I feel like I have jumped through the air. I hear the sound of tiny, tinkling bells.

"What was that, Grandmother?"

"That is your movement. That is your ability to become the stars and scatter your energy. There is no need for pain in the upper world, and your process of movement is in place now. You must remember on Earth there is no gain without pain. But in the spirit world, you are movement."

I feel light and soft. "Grandmother, how will I teach? What will I teach? Maybe it's best to marry and have children. I'll have a house full of children. Twelve, maybe. I'll marry a strong man, and we'll have a large family. Then I can teach. That will be the way of my teaching."

"No. No, Granddaughter, the ways of your teaching are that of Rainbow Medicine. You will teach of the seven stars. You will bring to the two-legged the Spirit Medicine. You will bring to them from the South gate the emotional medicine, the Dance of Seven Stars. You will bring to them from the West, seven medicines, a circle of medicine. You will bring to them from the North, seven stars, the medicines of the Mind. You will then stand in the East and honor the lessons. You will look up the road of lessons and share the teachings, and they will become taught. Then the lessons will have become teachings. You will do this again for the lessons of the emotions, and again for the lessons of the body, and again for the lessons of the mind. Then there will be the Footsteps and the Song. And there is more. The Impeccable Journey. These things are yours to have, from me."

I look into my vision's face and I feel at home. I feel at peace with constant. I sit now, in a point of energy. Now. Sacred spiral of constant. This is what I hear.

I find myself inside the rose hut, on a comfortable bed with a silky buffalo robe, nestled away. Underneath me is a blanket of many colors. I sleep, to the tune of the flute, the soft sound of the flute. As I sleep in the upper world, seven spirits dance around my head: the spirit of red, the medicine of Confidence; the spirit of orange, the medicine of Balance; the spirit of yellow, the medicine of Creativity; the spirit of green, the medicine of Growth; the spirit of blue, the medicine of Truth; the spirit of purple, the medicine of Wisdom; the spirit of burgundy, the medicine of Impeccability. They dance around me; they circle and sing. All night they sing and dance. Each medicine becomes four moons. There are four red ones, four orange, four yellow, four green, four blue, four purple, and four burgundy ones. Now their color spirals around me — the point of white and blue. I become the point, the center.

30

The moon sings to me. Six colors come from beyond it and swirl around me; then a seventh joins them. From the seven colors, four come forth—red, green, blue, and white. These four are directions; the seven are the stars. All is a spiraling wheel. It settles in my mind. Then quietness. I sleep in darkness.

It is morning. Skunk, deer, elk, beaver, otter, kingfisher, raven come—owl, hawk, heron, duck. Raccoon, small cat, wolf, coyote, bear, grouse, pheasant—all come—ant people, spider people, crawlies. Everything in camp sings, joined by the wind, the crackling of the fire, and the deep, calm, solid stillness of the earth. I come out to the fire. Grandmother Vision is not present anywhere, just the animals, their laughter, their joy. Fish jump as the water rushes by. I feel the peacefulness of nature, of living in balance with nature. This is a beautiful way to start a day! It is a good day to live.

I hear an echo: "It's a good day to die." "It's a good day to live," echoes back. Back and forth, "A good day to die." "A good day to live." There is a gate, made of two sticks in the ground. On one side of the gate is a red bandanna, on the other a blue.

"Come here."

"Go away."

"Come here."

"Go away."

I start to walk towards the gate. The closer I get to the gate, the darker it gets on the other side. A raven lands on the gatepost. "Are you ready, Wolf? Are you ready to teach?"

"Come here."

"Go away."

I look at the raven. It lands on my shoulder. "I'll walk with you. I'll protect you. I'll guide you. I'll be with you. I'll help you fly when you can only walk. Be careful. We must stay out of the void."

I hear the soft sounds of the flute calling me back.

These words you have read are real. They are a communication between my spirit and my two-legged existence. They come to me through spirit journey. I feel it is important to explain the term Spirit Medicine to you.

Spirit Medicine

First, of course, is the definition of "spirit." I define spirit as intelligence beyond the physical. Let me describe the word "medicine" to you. It is confidence; it is commitment, obedience, discipline; it is aid; it is change and health, alteration and rearrangement. It is an amplification of faith with the truth of what is so for you—for example, how your chemistry lines up with the chemistry of the product you place in your body. Medicine is finding vibrational frequencies and reading them. Medicine is understanding why we do what we do and using this knowledge on our path, so that we may achieve companionship, relationship, responsibility and accountability.

Spirit Medicine is relationship and communication with your spirit, which is your higher intelligence. Many times in life we overlook the clear, pure way of our spirit and follow our lower, smaller, physical mind. In Spirit Medicine we reach beyond physical limitations and push on into wholeness.

Teachings of Memory

It is important, when you have a vision, to get a full sense of it, to be able to interpret and understand it. From the vision of the sun, the moon, and the seven stars I have brought forth a memory—a memory of the voice of my spirit. It is important to remember when you are seeking out your spirit voice, your spirit eyes, your spirit walk, your spirit mind, that you never question what you see or what you hear, but only that you make sense of it. Over the years I have made sense of my vision. Grandmother Vision is my voice, my inner voice. Some would call it my guardian angel. My vision is my spirit keeper. I can't say that vision is a spirit keeper to everyone—but to me, it is.

It is important on your daily Earth walk to make sense of your memories. In order to start, I would like you to make a list of memories. Keep it in your journal, and every time you have a memory, write it down. Some people say it is a waste of time to remember yesterday, that it is not important to dredge up old memories. I disagree. The voice of your spirit would not call you to remember if it were not important. What is a waste of time is to beat a dead horse. It may seem useless to dwell on events that are over, but a memory is a haunting, and it is important in the teachings of memory to listen. Pay attention by journaling every memory you have.

Then start the process of putting them to rest. Sit with each memory. Think it through. Ask yourself if it is a part of now, or was it a part of then. When a memory is a part of then, it is haunting you and it is important to let it go.

To put a memory to rest, you'll need to run water. Go to a sink or a well, or a pump, and run water. Next take a glass, think of the memory and run the water into the glass. Then dump the water out. When it's gone, let the memory be at peace. When a memory is at peace, it is a joyful thought. It's important in the teachings of memory to learn to make everything a joyful thought. The bad memories, the good memories—let them all become joyful thoughts.

The Process of Knowing

These ceremonial processes may be done at any time of the day. Find a quiet space where you will not be disturbed, where there is no electricity, no noise, no interruptions, no four-legged or small ones to run through your sight—no disruptions.

Ceremony of Memory
The Ways of Your Inner Heart (the Spirit)

Tools: *Rock salt; crystal; 50 white prayer ties; 5 white candles; a rattle; sage and sweet grass.*

Take a long piece of yarn and tie each prayer tie onto it, so that you have a long, continuous line of prayer ties. After you have strung 50 prayer ties, you can wrap the line around a stick to carry to your ceremony, or just lay the prayer ties at your altar or on the ground where your ceremony is taking place.

Find a place that is quiet for your ceremony. It can be indoors or out. If it is indoors, place your medicine blanket on the floor. If it is outdoors, make sure it is a place where you don't mind putting down rock salt, because it may damage or destroy grass. It is best to be on dirt, or use

Making Prayer Ties

Supplies needed: *Cloth or colored paper; tobacco; red yarn; medicine blanket; sage and sweet grass.*

A prayer tie is made by cutting a one-inch (2.5cm) square piece of 100 percent cotton red cloth or colored napkin paper in red, orange, yellow, green, blue, purple and/or burgundy. When you have cut the square, place a pinch of tobacco, sweet grass and sage in the center of it, mentally placing your prayers in with the tobacco. Then, pull the corners up and gather them in. Tie the red yarn around the top, making a pinch bundle. Make 50 prayer ties at a time.

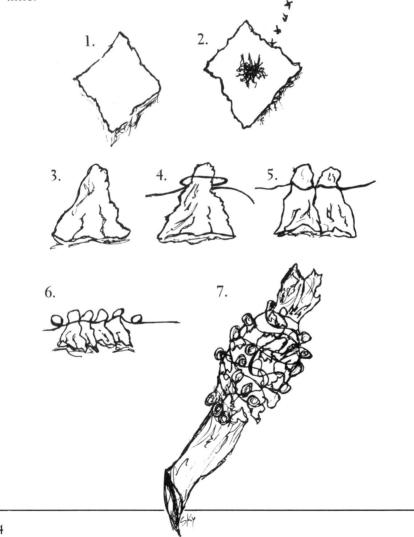

your medicine blanket, carefully cleaning up and removing the salt to a safe place after the ceremony.

Make a salt ring big enough to sit in, using rock salt. Mix pieces of crystal in with the rock salt as you make the ring. Start the circle in the East and lay your salt down as you walk clockwise. This circle is a sacred circle—a place where you are safe. The salt closes the door of spirit, so that nothing negative can enter. Only positive energy and light can come inside. The crystal magnifies this power and protects you in a way that is safe and comfortable, stopping all dark, unwanted spirits from coming in and out as you go through the ceremony. You want all your memories to be clear and clean. You want them to go back before the time of choice, before darkness, before evil. You want to remember when you were a bright light, part of the white light, part of the spirit world of light.

When you are finished making the circle, you will notice that it resonates a soft whiteness. Pale blue light will emerge around you. Then you need to smudge with sage or sweet grass, using your hand or a feather to move the smoke all around and through you (see page 20). Sit in the center of the circle with your five white candles. It is okay to place the candles in holders for safety. Light the candles in honor of Great Spirit Grandmother/Grandfather, in honor of any belief that you walk with, be it Judaism, Christianity, Buddhism, or any other system. All religions are welcome within the circle of light. All dark religions or beliefs will stop. There may be no dark religions within this ceremony—it is a ceremony of light. Only goodness can prevail in the ceremony of memory—no harm, injustice, no wrong or sadness, no deceit or ugliness, no disharmony or confusion—only the ways of light. With these thoughts you light your candles. As you light each one you are bringing forth a point of the star. The five points represent human existence, for you are a star. Each of us, as a human being is brought through in the form of five points: our head, our two hands, and our two feet. We need to remember that we are stars, for it is the time of the star people. We have come together in this ceremony in a good way, to walk the Rainbow Path and to listen to our memory.

After you have lit the five candles, take in a deep breath through your nose and exhale through your mouth. Do this four times, and relax. You will see a darkness in front of your eyes as they close; then you will see a familiar path, one that you will know to be comfortable to you. It is in your mind's eye that you will see this path. It will be some place that you walk that is familiar. Follow that path in your mind and it will take you through the corridor of your soul. You will enter into the spirit world, which is known as the upper world. As you breathe, begin shaking the rattle. Keep the rattling going. You are asked to see your very first memory, to remember the band, to remember the color. You are asked to remember; what kind of flower do you see? You are asked to remember, what kind of rock do you see? What kind of plant do you see? What kind of animal? And what kind of person are you? Remember these things and bring them back with you. Bring your thoughts back to yourself, towards the rattle. Come back in through the corridor of your soul, within the thought of your mind, into yourself. Take a deep breath, rattle the rattle four times, and move to the end of the ceremony.

Thank Grandmother/Grandfather, Great Spirit, the spirit of Christ, and all that is so for you, and blow out the white candles in the order they were lit. Leave the circle set up if you wish, so that you can come back to it to connect to memory. You will have already taken care not to place the circle where two-leggeds or four-leggeds will disturb it, but remember that all things that happen have a voice and wish to speak and teach you.

After the ceremony, write all the memories you have experienced in your spirit journal: the rock that you saw, the tree that you saw, the color that you saw, the flower that you saw, the animal that you saw, the you that you saw, and a star that you saw. Remember the color of the star. Record this as a spirit entry of memory.

The Medicine Blanket

Your medicine blanket is used to bring you physical connection to spirit. It provides safety and protection—through comfort—within its array of colors and texture. It is recommended that it be hand-made of any cloth of 100 percent cotton or wool. To care for the blanket, honor it every full moon by rubbing in the seven sacred disciplines—which are earth, water, ashes, sage, tobacco, sweet grass, and cedar.

Your medicine blanket is to be used in ceremonial work as a shield of safety. You can also use it to make a study bundle in which you can carry your drum, rattle, notebook, and things like that to class. You can use it at home on your bed, or take it with you at all times, even when you're travelling (put it around your shoulders in the car, train, or on a plane), or going to the hospital.

Now you have the memory of your totality, the knowing of yourself. There is an acceptance that comes now, a need to accept. It is here that you will find the medicine of memory. It is a medicine that it is very possible for you to have. It allows you to escape your fears. It allows you to resonate your fears, to balance them, and to come to grips with the fact that there is life beyond the human form—that you are spirit then, now, and forever. It is important to identify with the totality of yourself, for then you can honor yourself by having yourself flower, by having yourself plant or tree, by having yourself rock, by knowing the self animal, by having the self—the male or female—human. You honor yourself by knowing the band color, by having your clan, your spirit, star, color, knowing the animal side of yourself. The animal side of the self has the spirit clan energy in it, its wholeness. And the same is true for the flower, plant, tree, or rock.

Often people say, "Oh, I'm just making this up." I would like to remind you that the mind makes everything up. The mind interprets all thought; it brings forth all thought. Your child was made up: you thought it forth. Your work was made up: you thought it forth. Everything that you are is thought, which is manifested and made material, which makes it physical. So if you feel that you are just making this up, remember that you are going beyond fantasy. You are making a reality happen.

Acknowledging Your Memories

Tools: *Cornmeal; sage or sweet grass; spirit journal and pen; sacred tools of your choice.*

You will be building a cornmeal circle. Start by honoring the sun, standing in the East, where the sun rises. Raise a pinch of cornmeal above you, giving thanks to the spirits of the East and to Great Spirit for all that comes from the East. Honor the eagle, the spring, the morning and the beginning.

Now make the cornmeal circle seven feet (2.1m) in diameter by spreading the cornmeal clockwise towards the South. If you have chosen to work indoors, you may wish to spread a large blanket to build your circle. Once you come to the South, pause and honor the South in the same way. Continue forming the cornmeal circle, stopping to honor the West and the North, and moving back to the East gate.

Now light the sage in a bowl and, with your hand or a feather, move the smoke from the sage all around you. Offer the sage to Creator, to Earth Mother, to the four directions, and move the smoke over your head, past your heart—all around you—to remove any negative vibrations.

Now step inside the circle through the East gate, taking along your spirit journal and a pen. The realization of knowing the self has four parts: spirit, emotions, body, and mind. This means going all the way around the circle, understanding these four parts of the self. Once you step inside, do not come out until you have completed the circle.

1. **Centering.**

   Take a deep breath in through your nose and out through your mouth. Center yourself by sitting in any position you have learned, using any breathing method you have learned. I recommend extending your arms to the heavens and honoring Grandmother/ Grandfather, Creator, and any personal deities and spirits who teach you of the spirit way. Breathe in through your nose and out through your mouth four times. Relax and clear your mind. Become focused on the process of finding your breath. It is important to breathe slowly and evenly.

2. **Path.**

   We are going on what is known as a guided journey. It is shamanic journeying. Close your eyes, relax, and take deep breaths in and out a few times. To find your path, you need to use your imagination. It will feel at first as if you are making things up. Remember that everything we do, everything we have, and everything that we are comes through the process of "making it up." Making it up is thought. It is thinking it forth. You are going to think forth a path in your mind.

   You will start to see this path very clearly. It can be by the ocean, through the woods, in the mountains, on a sidewalk in the city; it can be along a street. The path is there. Your thought is very clear, and you follow the path. Allow yourself to hear sounds, smell smells, and feel feelings, as if you were physically walking on the path. *You are spiritually walking on the path.* The path will take you to a place known as your tranquility center. Other names for this place are your center of spirit, your spirit place. A familiar path takes you to a familiar center. You have passed beyond imagination and you are on a shamanic journey. You are journeying in the spirit.

   Your path will take you up or down. If you feel yourself rising, you are going to the upper world. If you go downwards, you might see yourself going into a hole, into a cave, going down through a flower, down through a hole in the ground. Going down will take you into the lower world.

If you remain on your path and feel as if you are going straight, you will be in the middle world and you are still in reality. You are actually having memories of now. You might see relatives, friends, or enemies, from your daily life. People will come to you on the path, straight into your face. They are memories of now flooding into your mind. When you are in the middle world, in reality, you can open your eyes and think about that, for your memories of now will stop you from attaining the upper or lower spirit world. So it is important to deal with things that upset you on the everyday plane that is known as reality. It is important to be at one with your reality. It is a part of your path, for your path is self: middle world reality, upper world reality, and lower world reality, as well.

3. Honoring memories.

When you have centered, taken your path to the upper, middle, or lower world, you will see a vision from that world. This is remembering. When you are in the upper world, you are in a space of being taught. You will have memories of where you have been as a spirit. Teachers, guides, angels, and celestial beings in the upper world will come to guide you. It is from the upper world that your faith is given to you. It is there that your teachers speak to you. You may speak to ancestors, and to the dead who wish to communicate, from both the upper and lower worlds.

When you are honoring memories, you are letting words be spoken to you. It is disrespectful to stifle memories. It is disrespectful to disregard the spirit worlds. Spirit world is memory, for it echoes the voices of your ancestors. You are in now, in reality, so the voice of your ancestor elders, the voice of your angels, the celestial beings—they speak to you from memory. They find ways to connect.

When you walk in reality, you are remembering the life of the ancestor who has walked before you. You are remembering the ways of your elder ancestors and of the energy from which you resonate. You are always, in your daily walk, living a memory. So honor the memory by giving thanks.

You will see yourself many times in the vision of your journey. As you sit in the physical realm, you may experience yourself speaking in memory. It will look like a movie, and you will watch it take place. Watch yourself honor the memory. There must always be a heartfelt thanks or honoring.

4. Understanding Memories.

When you have honored the memories, you are in a place of understanding them. When you are on your journey and in the spirit world, be it an upper, lower or middle world experience, it is important to understand each memory. Everything comes from all and resonates. Energy touches you and becomes reality. If it is a middle world memory, it could be an actual happening that took place in your life. Happenings resonate forwards, for they are constant energy until they are stopped. When a memory is put to rest, it no longer resonates.

Memories can be understood and put to rest by forgetting. They can be put to rest by forgiving. They can be put to rest by giving them away. You can give another person a memory once you understand it. When you understand your memories, you are in touch with your spirit keepers, the symbols of your guidance.

Example: Your spirit guide in the upper world is a cat. Cats represent sincerity and trust. Your memory is telling you that you are to apply sincerity and trust in your life, for seeing the cat brings forth the energy that is necessary for you to walk with in your daily existence.

Understanding your memory gives you solidity in the reality plane. Your life will not be a haunting at that point; it will be understood.

5. Interpreting the memory to now.

When you follow your path and go to upper world or lower world, the memory is experience. Experience is a reality within spirit world. All things that you see on a journey are reality that resonates into your life. In interpreting your memory, it is important to be responsible. Never play, conjure, or goof off with spiritual memory. If you are going to access memories, you need to know what to do with them. To interpret the spiritual realm is to understand your memory. Bringing the spirit memory and the physical memory together gives you your power. Interpreting memory happens through exploring its symbolic meaning.

Example: You see a tornado, a key, and a horse. You would interpret the tornado by what you feel, the key by what you feel, the horse by what you feel. Interpretations are always defined by teachers. They are also defined by your own feelings: tornado might equal power; a key might be opportunity or an answer; a horse might mean transportation. The interpretation of the tornado, the key, and the horse might be a powerful opportunity for movement.

Maybe your memory is just a sound of running water. Run that sound, or that thought picture, back into your life. This is your opportunity to interpret it.

It is easy to interpret memories by sitting with them. Your memories of the past from day one until now become clear when you sit with them on a daily basis.

Example: A childhood memory of abuse—someone slapping or hurting you. This is a memory of depletion. This memory flashes into your mind to remind you of having been depleted. Because you have not forgiven, it will continue to deplete you.

It is necessary to be at peace with all memories. It is necessary to have understanding in all situations. It brings about a closure. Interpreting is a closure.

6. Accept the voice of your memory.

It makes a simple statement. Accept it for what it is. When you look at the words "bad" or "wrong," the memory may be hard to accept. Look at the memory for what it is. See it as it happened. For example, take a car accident. See it as it is, one car pulling into another. Make it no more than that, no less. Then the memory can become what it is.

In accepting the voice of your memory, never take memories personally. The memories are speaking their truth to you in a picture that you will remember and understand in your life now. See them for what they are.

Example: I see a fence with a black and white horse jumping over it. Accepting the voice of my memory, I would interpret it as seeing a limitation being overcome. I would see the fence as the limitation and the horse as the overcoming. So my memory would speak to me of accepting and overcoming.

In acceptance your mind has the opportunity to rest. Then the voice of your vision can speak through your journey. A journey to your vision allows you to have clarity within your life, for you are going to the Face of Great Spirit, you are going to the Will of Great Spirit, you are going to the Heart of Great Spirit. And listening for Great Spirit's Will to be carried out in your life. Accepting the voice of your memory is interpreting it and living with that interpretation.

7. Giving thanks.

Once you have seen your memory, once you have obtained your tranquility center, your spirit keeper has talked to you and you have heard and seen everything that you are to see. When you have interpreted and understood, acceptance is at hand. Then give thanks to your memory. Be thankful for the opportunity to think things through. Be thankful to remember. Share a smile in your mind with your memory.

When leaving the vision, it is good to honor memories once again in the spirit journey. See yourself offering tobacco or corn-meal, giving red cloth or placing a bundle of sage at the feet of your vision keeper. Give a good thought to the memory as you make your gift to the memory-keeper—for the memory will bring energy to your daily life.

Ceremony of the Sacred Quest for the Spirit Self

Tools: *Cornmeal; spirit journal and pen; your medicine blanket; other sacred tools of your choice; sage or sweet grass.*

Build a sacred circle of cornmeal (page 61), smudge the circle and your-self, and enter the circle from the East. Lay down your medicine blanket and sit or lie on it. Get comfortable. Center yourself and relax.

1. Understanding self, understanding spirit.

In your spirit journal make a list of everything that is you, as many things as you can list. Include statements about yourself in a phys-ical way.

> **Example:** *You are tall or short, fat or skinny. You are bald or you have hair; you are female or male.*

This will help you to understand self. It is important to put down good things and bad things—things you do right and things you do wrong. It is important to see all sides of yourself.

Next, in your spirit journal, make a list of things that you are, ways that you see yourself, and ways you wish to live.

Example: You are a liar; you are a truth teller; you are spiritual—you're a wind walker; you are dead—you're a rider; you are alive—you're an earthwalker.

Brainstorm your mind and ask yourself to fill in the blanks. List everything about yourself.

Next, make a listing in your spirit journal about understanding your spirit. List everything that you can about your spirit: the color, the way it feels, how you hear it, what it longs for. List all the ways that you are in your spirit.

Example: Are you mean-spirited or good-spirited? High-spirited or low? Free-spirited or contained? Are you absent of knowledge about your spirit?

If you are absent of knowledge about your self or spirit, this is the beginning of your quest for your sacred self, your spirit self. You can open a door into the spirit world through journeying.

To have a better understanding of your spirit self, breathe and look for the path. Follow it to the tranquility center. Find a place to sit down. Ask your spirit to appear. Look in your memory. Look at your spirit picture that is happening in the upper world. Listen to the reflected self and understand the spirit voice of yourself. Know that all thought is spirit. Get a clear picture of spirit. Then you can formulate your actions, know, and record these actions as a list of the reflected self. This will be seen as a clear picture of your spirit self which will act as a guide for yourself coming from the upper world. It is pure spirit thought. Write down what you see.

Example: I see myself. I see myself with White Wolf. I have a wolf paw; I have a hand. I have white wolf fur; I have a long, white tail. My teeth are long; my face is human on one side; my wolf self is on the other.

You will see your spirit self. What color is it? What does it sound like? What does it look like? Bring your spirit self memories back and record them in your spirit journal.

2. Understanding your spirit emotions.

Understand that, when you are in the spirit world, there is no time; there is no day, no month; there is no season, no light nor dark—unless that is what is so for you. It can be sunny and raining at the same time. There are no limitations within spirit emotions.

Follow your path to your tranquility center and find a place where you can sit and feel the spirit emotions. Feel what it is to be able to fly, the feeling of being free. Feel what it is to be connected and full. Feel what it is to be original, to be ancient. Feel the memory of all—the emotion of constant. Remember these feelings and journal them. Come back and write more feelings about spirit emotions.

3. Understanding the need to connect spirit to physical.

Take the list that you have written about self and spirit self and draw a connection to how you gain from your spirit in your physical day.

Example: Your spirit is strong and solid and rich and full. Bring that back to your physical self and see yourself as strong and solid and rich and full, and write an affirmation: "I am strong. I am solid. I am rich. I am full. I am complete. I am rich, solid and full."

Build affirmations from your spirit knowing.

Example: "I am blue and blue is truth."

4. Understanding seeking the voice of spirit.

Learn to listen to your spirit voice. Feel the softness. Feel the warmth. Feel the gentleness, the completion, the original. Feel the totality. See the color, see all colors within. To understand seeking the voice of your spirit, you must begin to listen beyond your physical needs.

Example: Don't be so concerned about how much money you'll make, but how your heart will expand. Don't be so concerned about how others feel about you, but what your memory will be of yourself. Don't be so concerned about what you'll leave to your children when you die, but what you will be to your children always.

Journal your feelings from the four steps and see the value of questing for your spirit self. Understand your spirit, the spirit emotions connecting your spirit to your physical and guiding your physical with the voice of your spirit. Let the voice of your spirit set you forth on a quest. From the voice of your spirit you move forward as an understanding comes into your reality. From the voice of your spirit you have an understanding. This travels through your soul into your physical mind, where it manifests as actual thoughts. From there on, those thoughts exist. At this point you have an understanding of the voice of your spirit.

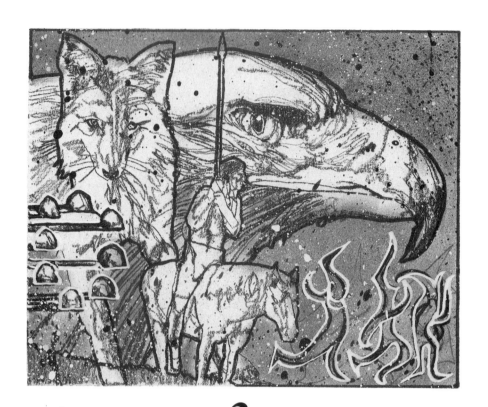

· 3 ·

RAINBOW
MEDICINE WHEEL

I am standing. I am. Now. All is consistent. Colors—all seven plus silver, gold, and white. All. Constant. Breathing in and out. I feel and am now the center. Accountable, responsible, sincere, honest, faithful, committed and dedicated. The center, now, me. I breathe in and out. Before me I see a gate. It is closed. Flags of colors line the gateway and on the gate is a red flag. It is within the Rainbow Medicine Wheel that these people come tonight. They come to find Spirit Medicine, to learn the lessons of the spirit.

I take a deep breath. My mind checks the room one more time. The burgundy floor invites their presence. A pillow to sit on in their color waits for them. It's time. A mystery school opens its doors. And as usual, two-leggeds arrive. Down that long path they come, full of excitement, in anticipation of learning. The smoke from the fire softly floats to the sky. My assistant is in place, waiting to organize, crowd control.

I breathe in and out. Before me I hear bells and rattles, drums. I straighten my black hat; the feather trails to the side. I take a deep breath in and honor Grandmother/Grandfather. What an honor it is to have the privilege to teach Spirit Medicine, to help people find a way to understand the depth of their spirituality. What a blessing it is to carry with me the wolf bundle, the teachings of the wolf—to be able to walk the wolf medicine. I hear Grandmother/Grandfather speaking to me in words from the color council, reminding me to reflect on all levels of the word "red." They remind me that it is red that we study tonight, and that there is more within the red—the shades of orange, and yellow and green and blue, purple, and burgundy. They remind me that, within red, each of its voices speak back and forth. I hear the caw of the raven—a memory comes as I look into its eyes.

I see the dark eyes of the raven that sits in the room. I see the earth medicine of raven as well as its personal totems. There are horses and deer, wolves and eagles. There are arrows and hawks. There are rivers and skies, bluebirds and coyotes. There are dancing spirits and a white mare. They are all present in this room. As the drumming goes, so do the feelings, spiraling around and around. I watch their eyes dart towards the bundle—beneath it is a Rainbow Medicine Wheel. There is curiosity in their minds as we drum and rattle—what's all that stuff on the wall? Their minds dance with the things in the room.

It is a lodge that we are in, a teaching lodge. We are now embarking upon the Rainbow Medicine Wheel, the mother wheel—the point, now. The song is constant. The gateway of spirit, the gateway of energy, the gateway of thought is the gateway of choice. Here are the medicines, the lessons, the images. Before us the weeks will go fast, the lessons will remain forever. We will build a bond, but we are not friends. We are alike, but we are not family. Those in this room will see each other, but not know each other. They are here to feel the sacredness of the Rainbow Medicine Wheel, from which their personal wheel comes. They are that personal wheel.

My voice dances around the room, and I feel it touch each heart. Their questions come back; my answers go forth; their questions come back. The energy spirals around the room. The wind blows softly. We are gathered at a spot beneath the pines; a circle is there, made of piles of stones, sticks, colored string, tobacco, cornmeal, with the smell of sage and sweet grass. This circle represents the sacred Rainbow Medicine

Wheel—the mother of all—the wheel from which all spirals into existence. There is a center rock, seven around the circle, four directions that form a cross. Within each direction are seven medicines and seven lessons. The gates are put in place; the prayer lines are strung; the torches and candles are lit. The dark of the night engulfs us, but the twinkling colors invite us between our choices and our callings. Rainbow Medicine Wheel has appeared; a classroom is in order.

In the center of the room on the floor the wheel is built. There are rocks, candles, and a medicine buffalo skull. Before us lies the Rainbow Medicine Wheel. We are in the center, studying the ways of the mother wheel. From us come many personal wheels. These are our prayers. We learn to breathe the wolf breath, the buffalo breath. Spiraling energy unites us with Constant. Thoughts emerge and Sacred begins. It is a goal to achieve respect through accountability. It is a goal to reach Sacred through responsibility. It is the utmost song to sing Sincerity. My voice dances and glides as the students quest. I see tears and release of pain. I hear laughter and joining hearts. I see glimpses around the room of people thinking the same thoughts.

Breathe in and out. The weeks pass. These are the teachings of spirit. We enter in the East, going past the red gate. We stand on the red stone, for we are in the direction of illumination. Face the East and honor the morning. The grand eagle circles above, spiraling, and lands in a large pine. The deer stands in the distance. We are the keepers of the East. We are illumination, we are gentleness. We are the majestic ways of Great Spirit, the corridor, the gate. The connection between physical and spiritual is soul itself. Through the soul is the corridor, the ancient road of memories, a connection between spirituality and physical existence. Breathe in the East. Remember I am the beginning; I am the Spring; I am the morning before the dawn. Sit with me and make prayer.

Each student has to tie twenty prayer ties a day, tiny prayer ties. They dance. Colors of red appear. Your clan is red; yours is orange; yours is purple; yours is blue. We are going beyond what we call Native American. It is a way, a blood, a memory. Native American is a label. We are going beyond that—way, way, way beyond that into the day of color. Before the four-legged and the two-legged. Before the winged ones and the crawlies. And constant is color. That is where we must be, always, eternally—heaven, beyond, now.

You'll need your spirit journal. You'll need to write down all your feelings. I want you to write what your religion is, what Great Spirit is to you. Then I want you to list your fears; list the thing that you are most angry about. Write every day. List your dreams; list your vision, the memories that you have of yourself. Every morning take time to breathe softly and gently in through your nose and out through your mouth four times, and then focus. Dress in your clan color, wear a shirt of your clan color in a loose cotton, along with blue jeans to balance the energy. Also wear 100 percent cotton clothing to tie prayer ties. These are the ways of the stars—to allow your body to be balanced in energy.

The students of the stars sit united, twelve of them. Their hearts beat hard. Each day is a moment in class. I listen. Weeks pass. We will light the red candle, the orange candle, the yellow candle, the green candle, the blue candle, the purple candle, the burgundy candle—to honor each color of star that guides us.

A breath in and out, and the room is dark with the exception of the white candle in the center, whose light twinkles eternally. It is time to hold the red medicine of Confidence. Light the red candle. The hand of the dancing spirit lights it. The red candle is lit in honor of Confidence, the medicine that we honor, Grandmother/Grandfather, Great Spirit, Eagle Feather.

When you are faced with the lesson of Patience, hold within your heart the memories of Confidence. The Dancing Sky speaks. The Faded Deer listens. The River Horse knows. The Quiet One cries. Each student in the room is given tests in his or her daily walk. Don't eat sugar, which will unbalance your mind. Don't take drugs, which will make it hard for your mind to do spirit work. Don't consume alcohol, which will alter your thought. Don't smoke cigarettes, which will harm your lungs. There is rebellion; they do it anyway. They pull back. They learn the lesson of Patience. Rocks are stacked. They speak. Do as the wolf says. The wolf lunges through the window and bares its teeth. The Frightened One crouches in the corner. "I'm not good enough." Child molestation, pain and agony. With abandonment and rejection come pain and agony. The black robes beat us down: "Do what I tell you." "Stand up." "Sit down." "Pledge allegiance." "Go home." "Come back."

Childhood memories are where we start. Be at peace and balance with those. Breathe in and out. I sit at the head of the circle in the North, on the buffalo robe, and listen. I watch them grow. From one who doesn't know who she is to another dressed in red with honor. Cover your shoulders with a medicine blanket. Be honorable. The lessons that you walk with are not about anything other than honor. Respect all things. Don't touch things that are not yours. Don't go places you're not invited. Don't open windows, and watch what happens when you open doors.

Confidence. Yes! Yes! Yes! "I can." "I don't have to." "I don't need to." "I'm not going to." Students say funny things. Words go around the circle, around and around and around. Evenings pass and they walk in and out of the wheel. I see these two-legged come in that gate in the realm of spirit. They're learning to listen. Their physical minds listen to their spirit. Their spirit says, "Slow down, walk carefully. Come in the East gate, honor the center, Grandmother/Grandfather. Honor the earth, the rainbow, and give from your heart. Face the East, walk the wheel, honor the colors, the words to come. Confidence, Balance, Creativity, Growth, Truth, Wisdom and Impeccability.

I see them sit in a wheel and pray. The lessons of Patience: Don't get ahead; don't get behind. Stay right where you are. One rock at a time. Putting things in order is how you learn the lesson of Patience. As you lay one flat rock on top of another, listen. The spirit person speaks. The one student with the shaky hand. The one who lies, holds things back, doesn't journal, doesn't want to do anything, doesn't even know why he comes. He stacks the rocks and they fall. "I'm not good enough. I'll never be good enough." The lesson of Patience is calling you.

It calls them to the room, where they spend the night, in the school. Maybe if I sleep right here, with the medicines, I'll get it. It's about following the teachings. "The teachings of Confidence are self love," I tell them. Your self must come first, with an understanding that you are one of two things—selfish or persecuted. I hear the words of Grandmother/Grandfather. They call me to the realm of spirit. I walk in the sky and look down. As students, they try. As humans, they're weak. But their spirits stay strong. "I can do it." I hear them say, "I can do it."

On their wrists they tie a commitment in red. The red candle is lit. Can you organize? Are you Organization? From the deer is a softness. It is a part of the spirit realm. Softness, Patience—must be a teaching. A quietness comes to the room, the gates are closed. The red candle twinkles in the night. I rest on the buffalo robe, reading the words that each one of them let go of. Standing in the doorway is the spirit of eagle. It is Eagle Woman, beautiful, full, and rich. Her face is part eagle and part human, her long black hair in braids. Her age is young, very young. She joins me at the circle. She wears a red belt, red beads. Her clothes are shades of the red rock.

"This is a good thing, that you have brought back the teachings of the red stars, that you carry forth the words of Grandmother/Grandfather. We are a continual movement of the cycle of life, in physical and spiritual. It is a good thing that you will be the teacher and there will be those who want to learn Confidence as a medicine. It is good that you will be the teacher and they will learn Patience."

The wind blows softly. I hear the frogs singing in the distance.

"Yes," she smiles. "The cleansing is happening. They're not so afraid

any more. They are on their way."

A softness in the room touches my heart. I listen. I feel orange shade into the red. It is time for Balance. A deer prances through the room, around the fire.

I hear the soft sound of the flute calling me back.

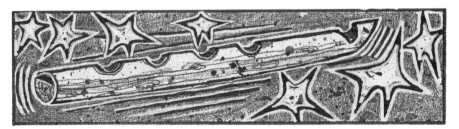

Teachings of Spirit—Confidence Medicine

The Lesson of Patience

From the red star, red is. The red is East. It is the doorway within the physical wheel of learning. The red is red medicine, Confidence. Red is also Patience. From the spirit we are united with our memory of consistency. We connect with Constant. The red teachings are carried on the wings of the eagle. A spirit keeper stands at the wheel in the early morning mist and speaks to us of deer medicine. Deer is the one who carries prayers to Great Spirit, Grandmother/Grandfather. Both deer and eagle give us the teachings of spirit. It is the memory of the Rainbow Medicine Wheel that is brought to us from the red.

A physical medicine wheel is a place where you can encounter spirituality. It is your own church, your own classroom, your own sanctuary. Medicine wheels are very old. Within the mother wheel that is mother earth, we have the opportunity to see all things, hear all things and do all things. The Rainbow Medicine Wheel starts in the center where creation occurs. A song of spiraling colors comes out from that center, and the seven rocks placed around it represent the Song. From the Song comes direction.

Starting in the East, with red, is spirit. In the South, with green, are lessons, emotions. In the West, with blue, is the physical. In the North, with white, is wisdom. In the spirit section, the East, are seven stones: red, orange, yellow, green, blue, purple, burgundy. With each of these stones are words of medicine: Confidence, Balance, Creativity, Growth, Truth, Wisdom, Impeccability. From the East gate, going into the center, are seven more stones: red, orange, yellow, green, blue, purple, burgundy. These are lessons: Patience, Unity, Original, Faith, Sincerity, Reason, and Worth. In each section there are seven medicines and seven lessons.

In the teachings of spirit, as we learn to be sacred, we listen to the Song, for we are accountable. As we learn to respect, we listen to the Song, for we are responsible. When we learn to pray, we listen to the Song, and we are sincere. When we learn to teach and we learn to learn, and we learn to give and take, we listen to the Song and we are honest. When we do, practice and be, on the good red road, walking in the good way, we listen to the Song of Faithfulness. When we select, when we make something happen in our life, we listen to the Song of Commitment. When we do it and carry it on, and produce it in our everyday walk, we listen to the Song—we are dedicated.

We apply our lessons and listen to the spirit keepers that walk through the gates. From the spirit, the spirit realm is carried on the wings of the eagle. From the emotions, it runs on the paws and the hairs of the coyote. From the physical, it is seen within the depth and the power of the eyes of the bear. From the mental, it is from the mind of the wolf.

It is yours, to build, to dream, to sit with, to have the opportunity to feel creation, to hear salvation, to walk with uprightness, to be on the red road, to follow the ways of Grandmother/Grandfather, great Spirit.

Building a Rainbow Medicine Wheel

The following instructions are for building an outdoor wheel that is large enough for you to move around in. If you don't have enough space to build a wheel this large, you can build a smaller indoor or outdoor wheel in the same manner and the same order; just decrease the size of the rocks and poles. When you use a small wheel, you perform ceremonies sitting outside the wheel.

Tools: *Rocks; poles; flags; votive candles in clay or glass holders; red yarn or cord.*

1. **Gather 68 rocks.**
   The center rock, the first one, is large—bigger than a human head. It can be crystal; it can be painted blue. The center rock represents Great Spirit, Creator, God.

Song Rocks

Then you'll need seven rocks that are a little smaller, about half the size of the first. These rocks are painted red, orange, yellow, green, blue, purple, and burgundy. They represent the Song and the seven stars. They are the first circle around the center.

Direction Rocks

Now you'll need four rocks that are not as large as the Creator rock but larger than the Song Rocks. They are to be
and white. These rocks can be those colors natu
paint them those colors, or paint them with symbo
colors.

Medicine Rocks

Next you'll need seven medicine rocks for each direction—four sets of seven stones, a full Rainbow. On each is painted a different color to indicate the medicine it represents. For example, in the red group, you'll have a red red rock, an orange red rock, a yellow red rock, a green red rock, a blue red rock, a purple red rock, and a burgundy red rock. In the green group you'll have a green red rock, and so on for the blue group and the white group—28 stones altogether.

Lesson Rocks

Then you'll need seven lesson rocks for each direction—another 28 rocks. They are to be plain. Paint a colored circle on each one to represent the spirit direction—red, green, blue or white—and in the center of the rock, paint a colored circle on each one in each of the seven colors, for the seven lesson words.

Poles

You'll need 12 poles. Eight of them should be from five to seven feet (1.5 to 2.1m) tall. Four of them should be three to five feet (1-1.5m) tall. These poles can be any type of wood, preferably limbs that have fallen from the tree naturally. Driftwood is good, or you can use wooden poles that you buy at a lumber store. These poles will become your gates. You have a gateway in the East with two poles, a gateway in the South with two poles, a gateway in the West with two poles, and a gateway in the North with two poles. Then you have a corner pole for the Southeast, a corner pole for the Southwest, a corner pole for the Northwest, and a corner pole for the Northeast.

Flags, Candles, Yarn

You'll need four colored flags, a red one, a green one, a blue one and a white one; four candles and holders in the same colors, and some red yarn for the prayer lines.

2. **Prepare the spot.**
When you set up a wheel, the rocks you collect should have a

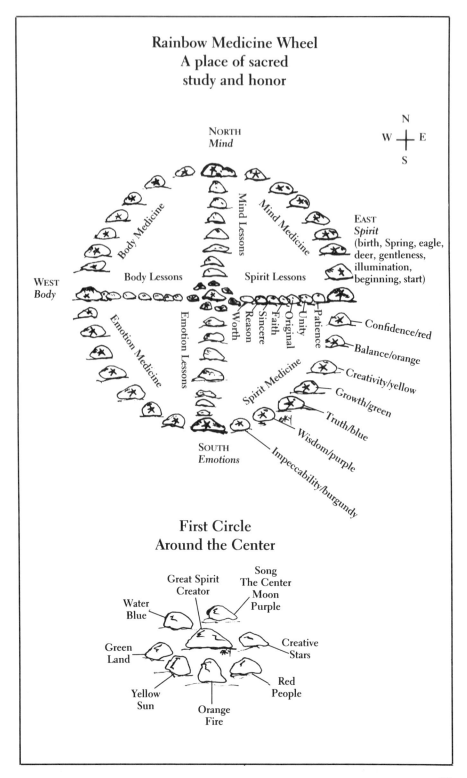

Rainbow Medicine Wheel
A place of sacred study and honor

NORTH
Mind

N
W ─┼─ E
S

Body Medicine

Mind Lessons

Mind Medicine

EAST
Spirit
(birth, Spring, eagle, deer, gentleness, illumination, beginning, start)

WEST
Body

Body Lessons

Spirit Lessons

Worth
Reason
Sincere
Faith
Original
Unity
Patience

Confidence/red

Balance/orange

Creativity/yellow

Growth/green

Emotion Medicine

Emotion Lessons

Spirit Medicine

Truth/blue

Wisdom/purple

Impeccability/burgundy

SOUTH
Emotions

First Circle
Around the Center

Great Spirit
Creator

Song
The Center
Moon
Purple

Water
Blue

Green
Land

Creative
Stars

Yellow
Sun

Red
People

Orange
Fire

special meaning to you. They must all be cleaned and free of negative energy. No anger or discord is to be connected to the place or the rocks chosen to build a wheel. To prepare them, smudge them by running them through the smoke of burning sage or cedar.

The place where you build the wheel is up to you. You are building a sacred circle, a place to go for spiritual strength and discipline. The spot you choose should be clean and raked. It can be grassy or plain dirt. If grassy, the grass should be healthy. If it is plain dirt, the dirt should be healthy. One of the best locations is by water—near a pond, river, lake, or ocean. The area you choose should be large enough to accommodate the number of people you want to have share your wheel. A personal wheel is four feet (1.2m) in diameter. A family wheel is eight feet (2.4m) in diameter. A community wheel is sixteen feet (4.8m) in diameter. The area above the wheel should be clear and open to the sky, with no branches or limbs covering it. The wheel should have an open and clear path to Great Spirit.

3. **Starting the ceremony.**
First, honor the ground with a give-away of cornmeal and tobacco. Take a pinch of tobacco in your fingers and hold it up towards the sky to honor Great Spirit; hold it down towards the earth to honor Mother Earth; offer it to the four directions; then place it on the ground. Do the same with the cornmeal. Offer prayers for the coming of spirits, for all spirits will come to your wheel. *Whomever you call will come.* Only ask for what you want.

4. **Placing the stones.**
When you have placed cornmeal and tobacco on the ground, find the center of your wheel. Place the first stone in the center to honor Great Spirit. Find the East and place the red stone outside the center. Following in a clockwise motion from the East and going around, place orange, yellow, green, blue, purple and burgundy stones, spacing them equally around the center. You have now brought forth the center, the representation of Great Spirit and the singing of life.

As you place your rocks, never turn around; always move clockwise to lay the rocks. If you need to turn backwards to fix something, move all the way around and come back to it, keeping the motion in your wheel moving clockwise. *Remember never to turn around; always move clockwise.*

Now set the larger stones for each of the four directions, starting by placing the large red one in the East. Place this rock seven feet (2.1m) from the Song Rocks; it represents Spirit. Stepping seven feet (2.1m) out from the balance point between the yellow and green Song Rocks in the center, place the green rock. This will be the South gate.

Stepping off from just a little past the green stone in the Song, directly across from the East gate, pace out seven feet (2.1m) and set the blue stone. This is the West gate.

Stepping out from just a little eastward of the blue Song stone, opposite the green rock, pace out seven feet (2.1m) and place the white stone in the North.

When you have placed the four direction stones, it is time to place your medicine circle. Starting again in the East and working towards the South, lay the medicine stones to form an arch in the section. It is important to remember that your medicine sections are going to build a total circle. So it will be East rock and seven medicine stones, red through burgundy, starting the East with red and ending up in the South with burgundy. Leave four inches (10 cm) or so between the last rock and the gate or South rock. It is important to remember that the four directions are gates and you want to leave the gates open.

Starting in the South, place the seven medicine stones, red to burgundy, starting with red at the green rock to burgundy at the blue rock. Then you pass the West gate (blue) rock. From the blue rock to the white rock place the seven medicine stones from the red rock starting after the blue rock to the burgundy rock ending by the white rock.

Pass the white gate and place the seven medicine stones starting with red next to the white rock going through to burgundy, next to the red rock of the East.Now you have built a medicine circle. You can true up your rocks and look at it as a circle, remembering that the directions are in the gates.

Now it is time to place the lessons. Return to the East, always moving clockwise in your wheel, and lay the red stone down. Keep laying down rocks as you move towards the center, where the burgundy stone will lie. Move now to the South gate. Standing in front of the green rock, lay the seven stones, starting with the red one, by the green rock and moving towards the center with the burgundy stone nearest the center. Now move to the West where you will be standing in front of the blue rock, facing the center. Place the red rock in the front of the blue and lay the seven stones, finishing with burgundy in the center. Move to the white stone and place the red rock, laying the seven stones with the burgundy one last to the center.

Now go to the East stone and step out behind it. When you look back, you'll see a center rock with seven around it, four large direction stones, a medicine circle of four sets of seven, and a cross in the center formed by four sets of seven. Your medicine wheel stones are in place. Now it is time to put in your gates.

5. Placing the poles.

Standing in the East facing West, beside the East stone, face the outside of the wheel. Take two large steps forward, stop, and dig a hole in the ground on each side of you. Place a five to seven foot (1.5 to 2.1m) pole in each hole, and bury them in the ground so that they are solid. They will form a gate large enough for you to walk through. Then move to the South and do the same thing. Repeat the motion of stepping back two feet (.6m), digging the holes and placing the gates. Move to the West and repeat. Move to the North and repeat.

Move on clockwise to the East and, staying outside the circle, step to the center of the space between the East and the South. There you need to dig a hole and place the southeast hold. Move to the South and repeat, stepping to the center of the space between the South and the West, digging a hole and placing the pole between the green rock and the blue rock. Move to the West and repeat, standing between blue and white rocks, digging a hole and placing the northwest pole. Move to the North and repeat, standing between the North and East rocks, finding the center, digging a hole and placing the northeast pole.

6. Tying the cords.

Now return to the gateway of the East and tie the red yarn or cord to the East gate left side pole. Move to the Southeast pole and wrap the yarn or cord around and then tie it to the right-hand South gate pole, standing behind the poles, on the outside of the wheel. Standing in the South gate, tie the cord to the left-hand side of the other gate pole. Still moving clockwise, wrap the yarn or cord around the Southwest pole and tie it onto the right-hand pole of the West gate. With the gate in front of you, facing the wheel, tie the cord to the left-hand pole of the West gate. Now continue clockwise, wrapping it around the Northwest pole and tie it to the left pole of the North gate. With the gate in front of you, tie the cord to the left-hand pole of the North and then move on, wrapping it around the Northeast pole and tying it onto the right-hand side of the East gate.

Now, stand in the East gate and offer a prayer for the lines that have been placed to form the circle, to enclose the circle, and to hold the energy within it. Say a prayer to represent the prayer lines, for this line is where you will hang your prayer ties, at your medicine wheel, when you study.

Always enter and leave the wheel through the East gate, moving clockwise around the circle. Only spirits use the other gates, not two-leggeds.

7. Placing the candles.

You now have the Rainbow Medicine Wheel built. You are standing in the East gate, holding the four candles and wooden matches. Kneel at the East gate, and place a red candle beside the East stone.

Then, as you enter the medicine wheel, raise your hands to the sky, shaking them gently to honor the Grandmother/Grandfather spirits. Turn to the East and light the red candle. Move to the South gate and place the green candle on the ground. Light it; rise and honor the South. Now move to the West and place a blue candle on the ground, light it, and rise and honor the West. Move to the North and place a white candle on the ground. Light it, stand, and honor the North.

Now move to the East, for then you will walk into the wheel, to the center. Light a white candle in honor of Great Spirit, Grandmother/Grandfather, giving prayers of thanks for bringing forth the vision of the sun, the moon and the seven stars. Give thanks too for the mother wheel, the Rainbow Wheel, where you have the Song of Great Spirit, Grandmother/Grandfather, Creator.

8. Placing the flags.

To finish your medicine wheel, place the East red flag on the left pole of the East gate. When you have tied this flag around the gate, it is open for the wind spirits to come and go. Place a green flag on the South gate, a blue flag on the West gate, a white flag on the North gate. These flags proclaim that these gates are open and the lessons of spirit, the teachings and medicine of spirit, the lessons, teachings, and medicine of each direction may come and go.

Your wheel is now ready to enjoy, to bring forth a memory that we are always a part of the Rainbow Medicine Wheel. All people are welcome at this wheel, all religions, all races, all creeds, for we are always, spiritually, within the Rainbow Medicine Wheel.

Using the Medicine Wheel

When you use a medicine wheel you should always be clothed. If you wish to wear sacred clothing, make it of skins or from free-flowing cotton cloth. It can be lightweight and airy, but always remain clothed while doing ceremonial work.

No drugs of any kind are to be brought into the medicine wheel. The sacred herbs, sage, sweet grass and cedar, the pinion wood, tobacco, and blends of sacred tobaccos, *Kinni-Kinnick,* can all be burned within the medicine wheel. You can carry potpourri and oils. There is to be no alcohol, no caffeine, no food, unless you are performing a food-honoring ceremony.

This is a place of communing with spirits. It is a place where the spiritual and physical become one in spirit. To honor the medicine wheel, never scream or yell in harshness or anger. You can cry out, extending your voice loudly to release an agony, but never become belligerent, disconnected, or hysterical within the medicine wheel. Distraught, argumentative, or disapproving behavior is not appropriate to the movement of the energy. You need to be centered at all times.

This is a place of respect, sincerity, and seriousness, of settling and coming to balance. It is not a place to make love or have sexual relations unless that were to be condoned by your teacher or brought forth as a sacred marriage.

There are not to be children running through the medicine wheel, or the four-legged. No one—cat, dog, animal, two-legged—should be so disrespectful as to run around the medicine wheel. You are to walk there in grace and respect.

If these rules are disregarded, you have been disrespectful of the sacred teachings of the medicine wheel. Each thing that is brought into this wheel is either a lesson to be learned or a medicine to bring good medicine to your life. Everything we do is within the wheel. We walk in the wheel every day; Earth Mother is our medicine wheel.

Your Rainbow Medicine Wheel is a place where you can sit and learn the medicines. Listen to the East, the section of the spirit, for that is where we are now. The South represents emotions; the West represents the physical; the North represents the mental. Studying first in the spirit section, your medicines are Confidence, Balance, Creativity, Growth, Truth, Wisdom, and Impeccability. Your lessons are those of Patience, Unity, Original, Faith, Sincere, Reason, and Worth. Enjoy your medicine wheel. Be sacred, respectful, committed and dedicated when entering. Aho.

Sacred Rock Stack

Tools: *14 large-size rocks; acrylic paint or water soluble paint; cornmeal; sweet grass or sage. You may paint the rocks—seven of them bold colors, red through burgundy, and seven of them pastel colors, pale shades of the bold. The seven bold-colored rocks represent the medicines and the seven pale ones represent the lessons.*

Building a Sacred Circle

Prepare the ground by cleaning the area. Build a sacred circle by sprinkling cornmeal, starting from the East and moving clockwise. Make the circle big enough for you and your tools to enter.

Before entering the circle, do a smudging ceremony. Light sweet grass and sage and move the smoke around your body; take it into your heart through your breath. Feel the earth and the presence of the four-legged, the winged ones, the finned, the crawlies, and all our relations.

Periodically cleanse your circle by smudging, moving the smoke from the sweet grass-sage mixture around the grounds and blessing the grounds through prayer.

Feed the sacred circle grounds by giving away to the four-legged, the winged ones, and all the other relations using tobacco, cornmeal, and seeds. Give away to your wheel, so that all that come to it give away to you. This is the sacred circle.

Place yourself and the fourteen rocks in the center of the circle. It is here that the ceremony of the Sacred Rock Stack takes place. You are called to listen to your rocks talk to you. You do that by stacking all fourteen rocks.

Start by breathing in through your nose and out through your mouth, very evenly and easily. Be at peace with yourself, for Patience is about peace. As you stack the rocks, you are getting the medicines and the lessons to line up with each other by stacking them in order; like this:

Listen to the rocks, as you stack them.

Whenever a rock falls out of the stack—or if all the rocks fall down—you need to read the stack.

To read it, you read what has fallen away. The rocks that fall out represent the things that you need to pay attention to in your life.

> *Example*: A solid red, green, and a solid orange rock fall out. You are being asked to apply Confidence. You are being asked to pay attention to your Growth, to things that are growth. You are being asked to apply Balance. This would be your reading from the rocks.

Start reading the rock that is closest to the bottom rock. If the bottom rock remains and all the other rocks have fallen, read all the rocks in the stack *except* the bottom rock. If the bottom rock moves also, it too is part of the reading.

After you finish reading the rocks that have fallen, continue to stack the rocks as an act of Patience.

When you have stacked the fourteen rocks—no matter how long it takes—leave them and let them stand until they speak. Your Patience is in the form of a teaching when the rocks are stacked, for you are patient. From the actions within your life, you know when you are being patient and when you are being taught Patience. To learn Patience, you must apply Confidence. To have Patience as a lesson, you need to act with Confidence. Listen to the rock stack. Its voice can also be used as an oracle.

> *Example:* You have stacked your rocks and Patience is at hand. You have a job interview to attend, and when you return home, you see that the rocks have fallen. You can start reading at the rock closest to the stack and there you will understand the medicine and lesson of the interview. If the stack is still standing, and no rocks have fallen, the interview was in a good way and the voice of the rocks is solid. There's a very good chance that the job will be a go-ahead.

If you should come to the rock stack to work with your rocks and they are all stacked, sit for a few minutes with the silence of Patience and remember what it feels like. Then take the stack down, mix up the rocks, and re-stack them. When you have a solid stack that has not fallen, where nothing has given you trouble, you have achieved the lesson of Patience. Carry this lesson into your life and read the stack from the bottom up.

The Order of the Rocks

The first four rocks on the bottom are the foundation. The next four rocks are the situations that you deal with, the things that you have to cope with, the things that you have to understand and change. The next four rocks are the growing and changing, the bringing forth that is necessary. The next rock is the balance. It is the rock that you have to come to grips with, knowing that Patience is obtained through Balance. The top rock is the outcome—the rock that holds the medicine and the understanding of the lesson you are learning within spirit. Keep this rock in your mind's eye. When more questions are at hand, or if you wish to work with Patience, sit with the rock stack and work with it. Always read your stacks in order, starting with red and then going to orange, yellow, green, blue, purple, and burgundy.

The Process of the Lesson of Patience

Tools: *Cornmeal; white candle; sage or sweet grass; other objects of your choice; medicine blanket preferred.*

Learning and studying Patience is done in a sacred circle built with cornmeal (see page 61). Smudge the circle and yourself, and do your prayers. Honor and give thanks for the earth, for the sky and for yourself, for Grandmother/Grandfather, and for the teachers who bring lessons into the process. Then step into the circle from the East. Sit comfortably in the circle with one white candle, which represents the Will of Great Spirit. It is to give light so that you are never alone when going through the process. The candle could also be a small campfire, if you are outside.

1. Sit with.

When obtaining and achieving the lesson of Patience, you are tried.

You are pushed and pulled. The pushing and pulling lets you know that you are in a lesson of Patience. There can be many lessons going on at one time. To achieve the teaching of Patience is to understand the topic that you are sitting with. This begins making you patient. Look at the topic. Question it to see if you understand where you need to be still and calm. When you become calm, the lesson of Patience is being learned.

When you are faced with a lesson, you are living it. In order to achieve Patience, it is necessary to be patient in every part of the self—calm, still, focused, clear, dedicated. Then you will have learned the lesson.

Feel a quiet deepening, a rich feeling, drawing you towards being centered and focused. When you are learning Patience, it is a restless and confusing time. When Patience is in place, and you have the first step of the teaching, the feeling is deep and rich. It is not unusual within the lesson of Patience to want to question, but you must remain in the *sit with* stage at this point. Otherwise, you will feel pushed and pulled, confused, unstable and disconnected. *Sit with* is still and deep, like a rock. You are patient at that time.

> *Example: Learning to bead is a process of listening to the elder who is teaching, be it a book or a person. Then you need to understand how to deal with beads—putting the beads on the needle, four at a time, and stringing them into the leather. Carefully, quietly, and deeply, you sit with the knowing of how to string the bead on the leather, repeating the process over and over and over, the same way.*

Similarly, Patience is a teaching you sit with and the actions are done over and over in a solid, deep way.

2. Organizing within learning Patience.
It is a faculty of emotion to organize and sit with things in acceptance. When you want to have something, you must be quiet and deep, solid in your spirit as you breathe in and out very softly. It is necessary to be organized within the emotions in patience. It will help to give yourself affirmations.

> *Example: Within beading: "I can do it. I will breathe carefully and watch my Elder. I will learn to put four beads on and then stitch the leather, then four more beads and stitch the leather."*

Knowing what you want to do, write out an outline of the process, saying, "I will put four beads on the needle and stitch the leather. I will put four beads on and stitch the leather."

This is the process of being organized through Patience. When we are challenged with work, we are faced with it as a lesson. Practice makes the lesson a learning. When we are acting on a lesson, the lesson is learned and then can be taught to another, and the lesson becomes a teaching at that point. For you know, and knowing is passing on. This is called "walking the trail." For teaching is the opportunity to face and celebrate lessons. In the Medicine Wheel, this is the lesson of life.

3. Affirmation.

It is important, while learning the lesson of Patience, to say, "I can." Give yourself plenty of affirmations: I will do a good job. I will give it my best. I will sit with and come with a deepening. I will not quit. I will watch my Elder, for it is attainable. When I draw from the spirit, I will listen to my vision and follow as it teaches me. I know that to get where I want to go, I must apply Patience. It must no longer be a learning, but an application. It becomes an affirmation in my lifestyle at that point.

Example: "I can do what my Elder tells me to do within beading. I will put four on and stitch the leather, put four on and stitch the leather." It is important that you understand that you will do your beading. You will be successful and follow your Elder. "I can do this. It is a good day to bead."

The affirmation of a good day will take you into the place of Patience as a teaching.

4. Walk with.

When Patience is no longer a learning, it is walked with. You walk with it when you have applied the medicine of Confidence. "I am confident that I can do it." When this happens, you will receive Patience as a teaching. Then you will be what you said you were. You will be what you sat with, what you organized, what you affirmed you would be. At that point you are walking with it.

Patience is at hand, a quiet, calm feeling. You are still and no worry is present. You are not in a teaching of Patience, but the lesson of Patience is at hand. To be "faced with" is a lesson, for you have the challenge of learning. When you draw on the lesson of Patience it is from the confident medicine within your spirit that you can do things. To apply Confidence is to stand and know. This brings a balance to your walk in life. You begin to place Patience in order and make it walk—be known and acted upon. Patience is hard. It must be applied or it will become a lesson beckoning you to take it and place it in order. To understand it is to apply it, to write it in your journal and show yourself how to make Patience a knowing. To make Patience an action is to walk your lesson, making Patience an outcome that everyone can see in your life.

· 4 ·

THE DANCE OF
THE DEER

The cracking and popping of the fire is the sound in the air. Smoke rises. I smell cedar with hickory, oak, and pine burning. The campfire welcomes the two-legged ones who seek out Balance, who long for the lesson of Unity. I watch them walk the sacred steps around the Rainbow Medicine Wheel, making prayer ties and placing them on the lines, pulling the breath of life into their body, putting themselves in a position of learning. This is the lesson of unity—learning to place Balance as the second medicine within their life.

I hear the prancing steps of the horse, the clicking, clacking, the soft deer movement, the meow of the cat. Each spirit has its sound and step— Dancing Spirit, Dancing Sky. They seek out the Unity, hoping to find the Balance that gives them self love, applying Confidence and Patience as a teaching. Joy fills their hearts as they join the rapid beat of the drum. It is time to dance the deer around and around the circle. We breathe in and out, in and out. Before me I see the deer dancing. I see the dancing spirits. I see the owls. I see the tree song. I see the spirits of students. I see two-leggeds eagerly calling upon their spirits. And I see the balancing. The point is constant. It is now.

There is swirling color all around. I am color; they are color; we are color. I hear the beat of the drum beneath our feet as the deer dance faster and faster, as a gentleness is brought to our spirit.

Cat medicine speaks to Orange and their ears listen. We are all sitting by the fire, listening to the orange spirits talk. Memories of constant are ours. Spirit speaks of all, both good and bad—of nothing, of everything, of something, of evil, of rich and full. The old lessons come to the voice of the teacher of the cat. The cats rub up against me and I pet them. The lessons of the bobcat, the mountain lion, the cougar, come as the cat people speak of ancient unity, a time before evil, when Unity was known, before dark. Then energy merged and resonated to thought. Thought became choice. There is always a choice. Within Balance there is choosing to, or not to. The evil things in life are simply choices. They might have been made in a split second, or they could have been made chemically before you existed as a physical being, but the choice is yours. The sparks of the fire fly high into the sky. I hear the sounds of frogs croaking in the night, "Croak, crack, croak, crack."

There is a quietness as the fire snaps and cracks and shifts, and the flames climb high. The old teacher speaks of a time when there were no Dark Eyes, when there was no evil. The Dark-Eyed One stands behind us. Once again I look into his face. I see a familiar spirit—the choice.

"Come here."

"I'll stay here."

"Stay there."

"I'll come there."

I look beyond the students and am beckoned by Dark Eyes. I want to leave the circle and go. I want to be consumed. I want to consume.

"It is your choice."

I look clearly at the ancient one who is speaking. It is a cat spirit. It has the form of cat medicine. I see the Old Cougar Woman telling stories of how it used to be, how it always will be. The black horse snorts. Dark Eyes disappears.

Yellow eyes are all around us. Each of us has our own eyes that we look into the fire with. The rattle shakes. We breathe in and out. Days and weeks pass, and lessons of Balance are at hand—standing on one foot, walking across the rickety board, breathing in and out—step down, step down, prance, step up, step, step. It is our choice to be in balance or to turn to the darkness that beckons us in the night. It is just a deeper shade of blue or purple or burgundy when we step into the darkness, the ancient cat spirit teaches. The grandmother leopard leaps quietly. The panther slithers. The deer prances and we dance. Blindly, we make our choices. We reach out for what we think is there and it disappears. Our unity must be achieved.

The stars swish past us. There is a glittering, tinkling sound all around and the snapping and crackling of the fire. In the center of the burgundy floor of the teaching lodge, the orange candle is lit. The orange tie joins the red one around the wrist. The process of Unity is understanding that there is choice—darkness, lightness, right, wrong. To achieve it is clarity, understanding, singing, forgiveness. Sometimes you'll step deep into the dark eyes of the panther. You won't even hear the cry as it devours you. I see the Panther Woman standing with the dark green eyes. We are a part of that medicine. You can't hold back any part of your humanness, for everything is you. There is lying and pilfering, raping and murdering. Two-leggeds are capable of all things. You can't stand back and say, "Not

me, I would never do that." Acknowledging the human is understanding evil—the dying, rotting flesh. Forgive us for we are sinners. It is the medicine of leadership within the mountain lion that shows each one of us that we have the chance to obtain our balance, taking one step at a time, not seeing with the physical eyes, blindfolded in the night. We each have the opportunity to act upon our faith.

When we see with our spirit eyes we look with Unity. It is our choice to step on the orange stars. It is our choice to listen for the balance in our lives. Moderation is the clue. It is the medicine of Balance to be moderate. If you are going to partake of the physical life, you need to stay in balance. Stay within limits, that's what the drinking laws are for. Stay within limits, that's what just one bite of sugar or two is about. When we partake far beyond our balance, we step out of our unity and we are faced with the dark eyes with the piercing redness in the center, with the snarling teeth. Out of guilt we rip our worlds apart. Out of disharmony and discord, detachment, and denial, we strike out for a title, a name, and beckon that name to come. We pretend we're something we're not.

The Panther Woman looks at us with a snarl. We're scared; we stand still. We're arrogant; we march forward. We're soft and gentle; we walk with the spirit soul intact. The doll of growth, soft green moss in her hair, the Earth, beckons us to come for healing. From our sacred selves, we choose, each one of us.

Long ago, in spirit, choice was born. Each one of us stands in a clear calling from choice. Crossroads in life await us and point to the spiritual or physical. All moments in life allow choice, opening us to lessons or teachings.

We prance and turn and spin, taking on the spirit of the deer, leaping out of the way of evil, staying within the spirit realm. We keep peace of mind within Balance. The soft night closes. The smells of sweet grass and sage linger in the air. Smoke floats softly down the driveway.

I hear the soft sound of the flute calling me back.

Teachings of Spirit—Balance Medicine

The Lessons of Unity

Within the teaching of the spirit of Balance Medicine and lessons of Unity, we are called upon to start the process of memory. The memories come. Life is a precious understanding of these memories. Echoes are a part of our existence. We hear faint echoes. We turn, and there is a memory. Why do we do what we do in life? What is it that moves us forward and pulls us back, holds us still and takes us forth?

Here in the spirit section of the Rainbow Medicine Wheel, we are listening to the ever-present memory of all—to the very point of now, within Constant, where all is color. That memory resonates in our minds. It brings forth, through spirit, a corridor we call the soul. The soul is like a hallway that allows the voice of spirit to come into our physical minds. Our physical minds absorb it and pass the thought back through the corridor of soul into the mind of Great Spirit. We have been removed from that mind, and it is within the medicine of Balance that we must recognize that this is our opportunity to have the lesson of Unity.

Unity is an acceptance. It is communicating with the dream world. Take your spirit journal, go to a sacred circle—a place where it is quiet and peaceful—and there examine your unity. Examine your balance. Make the following lists.

1. **Write your understanding of Great Spirit, Grandmother/ Grandfather, Creator.**

2. **List physical actions that you take upon yourself,**
   be they the rules of the Christian Church or the teachings of Rainbow Medicine, or the understanding of Buddhism or the traditions of Judaism, or any other religions or points of unity, calling you to Balance. List your religions.

3. **Write a clean, clear statement of what spirituality is to you.**
   Know the difference between "spiritual" and "religious."

4. **List your fears.**

5. **List your callings.**

Write your vision. Write down your dreams. Take the broken pieces of a shattered mirror and put them together, to bring forth an ancient drawing that is a path map, which allows you to see the totality of you.

6. List the whys.

Why would you kill? Why wouldn't you kill? Why would you harm? Why wouldn't you harm? Why would you lie? Why wouldn't you lie? Why did you? Why don't you?

7. List your recurring dreams and write your interpretations.

When you interpret the dream, write what colors you see, what objects you see. Look at what the dream is about (the points). Understand the different points within the dream.

> *Example*: *A dream of missing the boat. The points of the dream might be 1) that you feel lost or inadequate or a failure in your daily reality. 2) that the dream is a haunting, where you continually see yourself missing the boat. 3) that you see yourself turning away from the boat or walking away—giving up. 4) that you see someone stealing your boat and you're helpless to do anything about it. 5) that you see yourself continuing on— catching a plane to the boat—never giving up.*

Let the dream mature in your mind. This will lead you to a vision. Each vision will have its own story.

When Unity is in a lesson form, you have broken pieces of life. These are your daydreams, your night dreams, your nightmares— all asking you to listen, to pull the broken pieces of your life together. It's time to admit what happened to you. To obtain Balance Medicine, you must know what happened to you—what in your mind or in someone else's actions made you what you are? Within this space, ask yourself: Do I need counseling? Do I need to counsel? Do I need to find pieces of myself that are broken and shattered? Remember, Balance is the goal.

Pull together and strengthen yourself. Understand your clan. Your clan is a place where you sit and resonate. I walk with the clan of burgundy. Burgundy takes me through the lessons of physicality and lets me walk with Impeccable. Understand your band. Your band is where you fit into the totality—the absolute you. My band is blue. From blue I have my solidity. I stand out on the edge and look back into the fullest, truest, and purest color blue.

To make sense of this process, look at the lesson as spiritual. The spiritual point in life is strong feelings—your path, your heart thoughts. Make sense of life from being dedicated to the voice you hear through the lesson.

You listen. You give honor to the water and to the dirt. You go deeper within the cycle of spirit. You honor the seasons. From honor, the point you are in is solid. Your lesson is known. At this point of honor, your lesson becomes a teaching. For you have moved to the place of learning.

Make these entries daily in your spirit journal. Mark them orange. They are taking you to the flow of Unity. As Unity leaves off being a lesson and becomes a teaching, it is in place, because it has Balance. When you find yourself groping and grasping, cheating, stealing, lying, and pulling away, it is time to apply Balance Medicine, moving through the lesson of Unity, standing firm, and having it as a teaching. "I am. I have a shadow side and I have a light side. I acknowledge both and keep them in balance."

Spirit Soul Doll

Tools: *Glue gun; leather, 100 percent cotton cloth, 100 percent wool or 100 percent silk cloth; beads; natural objects: pine cones, rock, different kinds of grasses, herbs, sticks, root, sage; flower people to be dried or already dried; other objects of your choice*

To build your spirit soul doll, you will need to go to a scared circle, a place where you have put cornmeal down and smudged. The place should be quiet and undisturbed so that you can work with the structure of your soul doll. Take your spirit journal and pen. Enter into the circle from the East.

The Process of the Teachings of the Spirit Soul Doll

1. Path.
Breathe in and out, and see the path in front of you. Take that path to a familiar place that is quiet and peaceful. Within that tranquil spot, draw on your strength of knowing. Ask to see your spirit, to have your spirit shown to you. Pay attention to what color it is, what

type of things you see, what the symbols of your spirit are—to the animals that you see over four times. Anything you see more than four times is symbolic of your spirit. Note what type of animals they are, what colors, what types of smell, what oils can be used. What types of herbs and flowers?

Bring these thoughts back and journal them, to keep them in mind as you build the spirit part of the spirit soul doll.

2. **Soul.**

Breathe in and out. Sit quietly within the circle and connect to the corridor, the soul—the pathway from which the spirit enters the mind and through which the mind converses with the spirit. Stand in the corridor within your soul and listen to the sounds. Look for the colors. Feel the presence of what is there. What constitutes your soul? Remember the colors, the sounds, and the smells. Bring them back and journal them, to help with the soul part of the spirit soul doll.

3. **Honoring.**

Sit quietly within your circle and remember things of your spirit and of your soul. Bring these things forward and put them together, producing an honoring of spirit brought forth into form through energy and thought—by choice made into matter. Through the spirit soul doll, you will be able to communicate with memory.

4. **Sit with and listen to your spirit soul doll.**

Your spirit soul doll is yours to build and bring forth. Sit with it and work with it in a good way.

> *Example: When I sit with my spirit soul doll, I play the flute, burn grasses and listen to the night. I hear the stories of the voice, a deepening within myself. Thoughts of being a path-finder and leader, thoughts of carrying, shooting through the night, stories to the hearts of those that wish to hear. A deepening and quickening is mine when I sit and listen to the spirit soul doll.*

Making the Doll

First you outline your self, making a list of all that is you, how you see your self.

Example: *My spirit is that of wolf, of snow, of crisp and dark blue, light blue, stars, of things that are pale blue, white, shimmery silver. My soul has the smell of the river, the scent of nature. I smell pine and sweet grass. I smell lilac and lavender. I smell sage and tobacco. I see colors of blue and burgundy, with surges of bright white and yellow light.*

Bring together the things you have outlined, such as, in the example above, the wolf hair, little stars, and different oils.

You can make the body of the doll in different ways. You can roll up leaves, or different types of cloth or cotton, add bundles of herbs, and tie

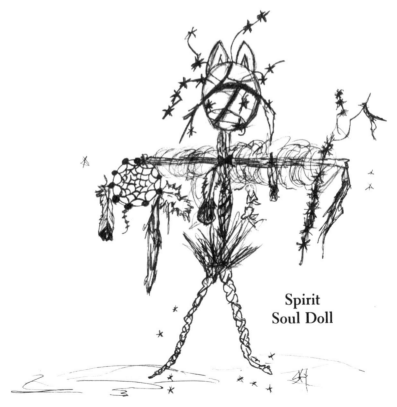

Spirit
Soul Doll

the whole thing together with string, to form the torso. You can roll up smaller bundles and tie them with string to form the arms and legs. You can make the head this way, too just by rounding the object into a ball.

Example: For my spirit doll, I use strips of shimmering yellow, white cloth, cut them very thin, and other cloths from light to dark blue. I wind wolf hair around the cloths. Then I rub the oils onto the dried pieces of lilac and pieces of lavender and put them on the body. I take string and tie on burgundy beads that glisten. I make the rest of the wolf hair into a ball to create the head. I put stars on for hair. I add shavings of cedar and sandalwood to guide and protect me. I make a small dreamcatcher and place it in my spirit's hand to remind me that I am spirit flowing through dreams. I have a finished product, a spirit soul doll.

The Process of the Lesson of Unity

Tools: *Tools of your choice; sage or sweet grass; your spirit journal and pen; cornmeal; drum or rattle; an orange candle in a holder; medicine blanket.*

Find a quiet place and give yourself plenty of time for thinking in the lesson of Unity. Build a cornmeal circle (page 37), a place of honor that you will enter after you have smudged. Take with you a drum or a rattle. You will need your journal and pen, and your medicine blanket to keep around you for safety and warmth, to keep you focused and feeling united. You can also have an orange candle to light, to bring forth the medicine of Balance, which is the orange medicine from the spirit.

Honor your circle in the lesson of Unity. Sit and become very quiet. Breathe in and out through your nose and mouth four times, and become relaxed, open to Patience. Then, using Patience as a teaching, sit solidly with it, clearing your mind.

1. **Clarity.**

   Feel yourself clearing and look at life. Look at it as a piece of flat dirt. Draw a line on that dirt in your mind's eye and stand on that line. The line represents Absolute, Correct, Clarity, Will of Great Spirit. Think about those words. If you see or hear anything, record it in your spirit journal, for it is a part of your Clarity, a part of clearing for Unity. It is important to visualize the dirt, with the line. On one side of the line, see the dirt as very dark. On the other, see it as very light. Remember which side is which. Record that in your spirit journal.

Making the Dreamcatcher

The dreamcatcher is a small hoop made of wood—a twig from any tree can be used. Its purpose is to capture negative thoughts or dreams. It may be hung in a window or by the bed on a lodge pole or on a dance stick.

To make a dreamcatcher you need one piece (fresh) of a green tree branch, small in size. The larger the branch, the bigger the hoop of your dreamcatcher. Bend the branch into a circle and tie it with a piece of colored cotton string that is about 50 inches (127cm) long.

After wrapping the ends of the branch together with the cotton string, tie the string around the hoop at about 1½ inch (4cm) intervals. It will look a little like a spider web. When you have reached the spot where you started, tie a second row in the middle of each swag. Each time you tie it, pull the string tight and then tie it to the next center. Keep tying and pulling tight, making row after row. This intensifies the spider web look. Pull it tight in the center. Tie a knot and let the rest of the string hang down.

Tie feathers or beads on the end of the string. This completes the dreamcatcher. Tie a 6-inch (15cm) long string around the hoop at the top, so that you can hang the dreamcatcher on a nail. Tie on a small piece of lavender for softness.

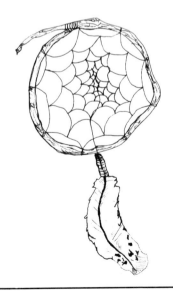

2. Undertake the Medicine of Balance.

Sitting in your circle, visualizing the line in the dirt, breathe in and out four times. Recognize the medicine of Balance as you. Is yours a life of obsession? A life of dependency? A life of approval and proving? Is it a life of being, giving and doing? Recognize the different sides of your life — the empty, the needy, the rich, the full. The rich and full is on the light side in the dirt. See things there that are rich and full in your life. Record them and put them in your spirit journal. The things that are empty, cold, and disconnected are on the dark side of your line. Record those things — the things that separate you from your point, that take you away from your goals, that keep you from being who you want to be.

See the difference between the two sides by standing on the road, the line down the middle. Look at the things that you live for in the light, and the things that you don't want to live for in the dark. You can place all philosophies in either the light or dark — your choice. You can place religion within light and spirituality within dark. You can place "following" within dark and "leading" within light. Come to an understanding of yourself, standing on the line of Clarity.

3. Sing the Unity.

Looking at the happiness in your life, hum or sing an unknown song, not one you've heard on the radio or on TV or learned from someone else. Bring forth a resonant song of tones, which is the light side of your wheel. It might be sounds of swirling wind and all you can do is a whooshing sound.

Now listen to the dark side. It might be a low, moaning, groaning. It might be grunts. It might be zigzags of sound, sharp rising and falling tones.

Sing the song of Unity by pulling these two sounds together, and bring forth a chant that is four repetitive lines of the same sounds, balanced between dark and light. Balancing the two brings forth acceptance. It shows you your direction. Sing the Unity. End the singing with a long hummmm sound.

4. Forgive yourself.

While sitting in quietness after your song and your circle of Unity, forgive yourself for all the things about you that you feel are inadequate. Open doors of new opportunity. Remember statements like, "I'll try harder. I'll do for myself what is necessary. I will go where it is necessary. I'll be what's necessary." Remember that opening doors of opportunity is looking ahead, down the road, knowing that Clarity is the line between light and dark. Understand that there is a line of absence and a line of support. Breathe in and out and see the line in the dirt. Look up that line and record in your spirit journal what you see. Come to the process of Unity any time you feel you need direction.

· 5 ·
ANCIENT SPIRIT
DRAWINGS

Before me, the sun sets. It is a quiet evening; there is a soft breeze. Colors of burgundy and orange, light blues, dark blues and purples fill the sky. Twilight is where I stand. Two-legged students walk the path to the Rainbow Medicine Wheel, tying their prayer ties. I see a stability about them, a strength that is growing. The sacred medicine blankets are around their shoulders; their clothes are the colors of their clans. Each one honors the mother wheel, breathing, flowing. The drum calls the familiar beat. I place my black hat firmly on my head, taking a deep breath of prayer, "Grandmother/Grandfather, Great Spirit. Allow me to teach the ancient ways. Give me the blessings to give to others that they might see within their spirit drawings a way through the woods, down by the river, that they may step and prance and dance as the deer, walk softly as the cat on the ground. Grandmother/Grandfather, thank you. Aho."

The Talking Stick goes around the circle. People are spirits. Their eyes show a longing for more memory of the spirit. Homework is turned in; the journals are good. People are following, making lists of 1–25s. Teachings of organization begin. Creativity is the topic within yellow. I've walked on the stars, and I bring the teachings of the yellow stars to us. I will share with you a vision journey.

Before me I saw a path in the dirt, and the dirt was yellow ochre. I followed that yellow dirt to a camp. There was a small tree house, a hut built within a tree, a ground fire, and a campfire ring. Chairs were cut from wood. On a tripod a pot hung. There I met up with a spirit keeper, Hawk Man, a keeper of ancient spirit drawings.

The sun was shimmering around his head, which was half man and half hawk. On his bare chest he wore a breastplate of hawkbones, the feathers of the hawk. Yellow cloth was wrapped around his hips. His arms were hawk wings. He stood with great pride.

Hawkman had me listen to the wind that blew across the ground and cleaned the dirt smooth. Symbols appeared in the dirt—blue and yellow, orange and red—made of cornmeal. There were little trays of cornmeal for me to draw with also. The wind moved my hands, and I laid symbols in front of me, making a drawing of the sun with four direction lines, seven stars, and the crescent moon. Behind it were some mountains, with a bird etching, pine trees, and a wolf dog.

"This is your ancient spirit drawing." I looked into the face of Hawk Man. He took cornmeal in his hand and sprinkled it on my drawing; then there were snowflakes dancing and falling into the river, and stars twinkling down over the mountains—you could see them above the pine trees. I looked at his face. The human side of him was so familiar and the hawk side of him so ancient. His body was a perfect blend of man and bird.

"I am the messenger. It is my job to open the door to your ancient spirit drawings. Here are your ancient ways; the stars are your footsteps. Through the sun you have come, with the energy of the messenger. We'll walk the stairway through woman and wolf. You are a messenger of the stars, one who speaks truths like water that flows. It is important to remember always to go downstream. Never struggle to go upstream; it is yours to go down, to go with the flow. The easiest thing for you to do will be to sit and teach. It will be as that cluster of rocks in the river: the water is separated—lessons are opened. The flow unites—teachings are in place."

I looked at my ancient spirit drawing and I could feel each word he said. "I want to sit with you longer. I want to know the ways of Hawk." He extended his wing and pointed to the sun. "Direction—East,

South, West, and North. These are your knowings. I am simply here to speak of this spot in time, the ability to create your life." I looked into the sun as he pointed to it. He disappeared. I was there alone with my spirit drawing.

Two people came, both female—one a Gypsy, the other an Irish girl. The Gypsy said, "It's time to make a map. From 16 to 36, your earth walk will be with one of these maps—from 36 to 56, with a second—from 56 to 76 with a third. The way of your mother is now in your hands." We drew maps together.

I looked into the shadows and there stood my mom, raven dark hair, piercing eyes. She held clutched to her heart a tattered map. It was making sense to me now. My mother had a sacred ceremony she followed always. It took her to the places that were real for her. She always spoke of never worrying when she went to bed, because she knew the way. My mind drifted back into the ancient spirit drawings. The three of us were sisters now. The Gypsy spoke, "Sisters, always, within the map.

The ways of the sacred voice of the wind, the corn, where vision becomes picture and picture becomes direction."

The Gypsy woman instructed me to draw what I wanted my life to be, who I was to marry, where I was to go, what my family was to be like. And most of all to draw tombstones and put smiley faces on them, so that I was in balance with death. For death was like a tombstone; it was a doorway. The shape of a tombstone, arched, showed me that it was a door. I opened the door, and as I stood in the doorway I heard the singing of children, the singing of birds, the smells of spring and fall. Beauty beyond words was on the other side. It was easy for me to understand death from that moment on. I had dealt with it within my ancient spirit drawings.

We spent the rest of the evening and all the next days together, drawing our future. The winds told us that there was no future, for there is no time. There are only footsteps and doorways. "Everything moves along as it should," Great Spirit says.

"It is important that we put things down in symbols," the Gypsy says. "Draw them in words and write them in your spirit journal, but then make these words into symbols and put them on skin, paper, or cloth and they become ancient spirit drawings, ways that you follow that take you through the twists and turns."

I was excited. My map was filled with all kinds of treasures. There were material things like jeeps and trucks; there were spiritual things like enlightenment and Clarity, introspection and Wisdom, innocence. There were homes, and places to see, people to meet. Lots of little yellow eyes peeked out from behind rocks. Books sat on the shelf. There were many things—things that were brought to reality as the years passed. The maps were signed by us as sisters, with the mark of the raven, the mark of the wolf, and the mark of the bells (or *Balance*). We rolled the maps and kept them sacred to our hearts, to come forth again next year. We signed the commitment together. The wind blew; the drawings scattered.

Back in the classroom, stories of the map filled the night. Students placed yellow cords next to the orange ones on the their arms. The commitment of Creativity was an understanding of creative visualization with ancient spirit drawings for guidance. These drawings are ways that you organize your life from Balance. Creativity is within the hands and the eyes of the beholder. The yellow candle is lit. The flame twinkles in the night. Excitement spirals in the room. Hearts beat clearly, loudly. Energy fills the room. Evenings are spent with needs and wants, thoughts of acceptance, having salvation by knowing, walking the Balance way, bringing in Creativity—understanding that a stick drawing is as good as a photograph. Creativity emerges in their faces. I watch the spiraling flight of a Chinese pheasant.

Creative visualization is theirs. Tomorrow is what they see. A quietness comes to the room. It is an evening of Dancing Spirit, an evening of Big Sky. Soft sounds of the Black Horse clip away in the night. I hear the song of joy within the lungs of the Bluebird. The River Horse gallops in the night. On the wings of this evening I feel that we are halfway. Halfway—red, orange, and yellow—together we have come three colors. I sit in the stillness of the evening, the soft glow of the red, orange, and yellow candles. I hear the bells, the drums. In the distance, I smell the smoke of sage. A quietness comes to the lodge. The learning of Creativity is a leap of faith. To be creative is a leap of faith. From yellow to green, we now go.

I hear the soft sound of the flute calling me back.

Teachings of Spirit—Creative Medicine

The Lesson of Original

Within the teachings of Creativity, within the spirit realm, the lesson of Original is to be learned. If you are to have Original in your life, it's like baking a cake. You'll need a recipe. You'll take a little movement, a little action, a dose of care, some accountability, some purpose. You'll apply Patience and Unity, put in Confidence and Balance, and before your eyes, Creativity will be birthed.

The lesson of Original is flowing. It is allowing yourself to be. It is important to remember, when you bake a cake, not to stomp and bang the floor and bump the oven. So it's important within learning the lesson of Original, just to be. The flow is what is so. Be careful not to alter it with visions of money. Be careful not to sell out to what someone else has in mind for you. That is like a bump or a blow to the floor and the cake will fall. It may still be creative, but it will have fallen.

If you've been careful not to bump your cake, and you've used just the right temperature—poof! Your cake will have a beautiful shape and a magical, sweet flavor. The center of a party appears. Creativity is the party. And from Original, our life is tossed and turned, flipped and spun, beckoning us to flow. Original is, Creativity produces. From the spirit realm, listen to the flow. Being creative is okay just the way it is. I think the most creative thing that Great Spirit, Grandmother/Grandfather has given us is a leaf that floats from the tree in the autumn—and the story of the elf that lies on its back and rides to earth, hitting the ground and scampering away. The beauty within the children's stories—what creativity from the spirit! Learning the Original lesson is going to constant, and seeing the swirling pattern that we are. The teaching of Original is applied when you understand not to separate, but to be.

Ceremony of Movement

Tools: *Medicine blanket; drum; a rattle; other tools of your choice; one white candle in holder; matches or a fire pit; cornmeal; spirit journal and pen; sage or sweet grass.*

This ceremony is to be done in the sunlight. Build a cornmeal circle (page 37). Smudge, and enter the circle from the East. Sit and be comfortable. Place your candle and open your spirit journal.

1. **Needs and wants.**
   Needs are spiritual and wants are earthly. Make a list of your needs and wants and enter it in your spirit journal.

   Example: Needs—communication with spirit through journey, prayer tying, nature, the lessons, and the beauty of nature. Wants—a nice truck to get to a place in nature where I will be undisturbed; a tepee to set up and make my home while I enjoy nature and listen to spirituality.

   Your needs and wants are lists that will be essential when you make your ancient spirit drawings, your path map. Write down everything that you need and want, because as you write it down you bring it forth. Understand that wants come from needs. Your needs are points of enrichment that allow you the ability to want.

2. Clarity of spirit—the calling.

Light the white candle. Make a circle around it with cornmeal. Do 50 prayer ties in honor of needs; make them in white and purple. Do prayer ties in honor of wants; make them in red and blue. As you make the prayer ties, listen for your clarity of spirit. Listen for your obedience, for your purpose. Your spirit carries with it the ancient records of Original. Being is enough, for clarity from the spirit brings about clarity in the physical.

3. Clarity of spirit—1–25.

Often we feel we are not enough in life, and we do not look at the fullness of what we are. Make a list, and at the top write 1–25. Then list 1 through 25 down the left-hand side of your page. Next to these numbers, list 25 things that you hear in clarity from spirit that you are. List things that are relevant to your life.

Example: Human being, woman, wolf spirit, daughter, sister, wife, mother, grandmother, author, writer, spiritual teacher, visionary, shaman.

Record this list in your spirit journal.

4. Purpose—1–25.

Make a 1–25 list that shows your purpose in life. Draw a line down the page and on one side put "good" things of purpose, and on the other side put "bad" things of purpose.

Example: On the "good" side—voice, teacher parent. On the "bad" side—one who stirs, one who drives out, one who demands.

Often the things we look at as bad are things that bring about change—"one who stirs," for example. When we look at things like one who rapes, one who murders, we all are guilty. For example, everyone kills—we kill bugs, we kill food to eat. Try to take things to the core; one who kills is "one who removes."

We are accountable and responsible for every sincere action that we honestly bring forth through faithfulness and by being committed and dedicated in life. But it is our resonance to look within the good *and* bad. List your purpose as a life of good. Put the things that fill you with guilt on the "bad" side of the page and take them deeper. Everyone is guilty of moving life from one space to another. For you to have your wholeness and for you to have your process of Creativity, you must bring your purposes into one, as a life of good.

After you have looked at the two sides, good and bad, bring them to a core. Make a list of your abilities:

Example: *Clear and open*
Able to make changes
Have the ability to be original
Can bring about clarity
Have a voice to be heard
Have awareness
Have the ability to work hard
Can bring transformation to share with all
Have the ability to teach

Then find the energy of your purpose as a life of good, and bring your statement of purpose into its wholeness.

Example: *I am a voice who stirs. I bring about change in life. I give opportunity to Original to seek out clarity within the pattern. I am a voice in the night who calls to awareness, bringing forth vision and transformation. It is my opportunity to share Original with all those who wish to make it a teaching.*

5. Action of movement—acceptance.

As you sit in quietness with the candle, make a list of 1–25 describing movement within your life.

Example: *Change was brought to me, and I was given no choice. My parents' will governed eighteen years of my life; their habits became my habits. Their teachings were my teachings. Then I chose to fly with my own wings, to walk with my own feet. I separated from everything that was theirs, putting it over there in a pile and me over here in a circle. I chose to take my mother's stamina. I chose to take my father's perfection.*

Narrow down the items in your list of 1–25 to single words: stamina, hardheadedness, stubbornness, fear, success, perfection, honesty, humanitarianism, for example. List the movements that have taken place in your life, from as far back as you can remember—both light and dark. After you have listed these things, sit with them and look at how your life has been affected by others: how school affected you—high school, junior high, college—how church affected you, how going to the grocery store and shopping affected you. Include what friends meant to you, places where you were put upon by others. It's important to list all these things in your 1–25s.

As you sit with your list in the quietness with your candle, look at why you need what you need. Spiritually, your needs are solid. Look at why you want what you want. So often, we can see that what we wanted to be was someone else. You might be able to look within your childhood and see that your parents always wanted to play golf and couldn't, and that's all you heard about, so you carry it forth in your adult life thinking it's what you want to do. You might have simply followed someone in their grandness; perhaps your parents were champion billiards players, so you are too—like mother, like daughter, like father, like son. Find an acceptance and, most of all, bring forth your balance. Have the confidence to ask yourself if your needs and wants are yours or someone else's.

When you are sure about this, look back at your needs and wants and list only those that are yours. Put them into motion for you, for you accept them.

Ancient Spirit Drawing—Path Map

Tools: *A piece of 100 percent cotton cloth, paper, or deerskin—as large as you wish; more paper; spirit journal and pens; beads, sequins; paints, sage or sweet grass; and other objects of your choice.*

This ceremony is to be done at night. Start by smudging all the things you are going to use by passing them through the smoke of sage or sweet grass. On the skin, cloth, or paper you will build a drawing that is your personal map that will cover the next twenty years. It will bring forth your ancient spirit drawing.

1. Creating symbols.

From your needs and wants list, take the words and turn them into symbols.

Example: A jeep. Make a pictograph, a little drawing of a jeep.

It is important to write down these needs and wants in your spirit journal and to put the drawings out beside them so that you can identify them later.

2. Creating the path map.

In a ceremonial setting, such as a cornmeal circle (page 37), enter from the East and sit with the objects you have chosen to put in your map. You will be drawing your symbols and painting them on the paper, skin, or cloth with permanent paints or markers.

Start by making a large circle on your drawing area. Show that your spirit enters from the East and honor the East gate on your drawing. Place a symbol for the Creator, Great Spirit, in the center of the drawing, representing your faith, religion, and spirituality.

Your map should move in a clockwise circle. You can mark it off in sections of color to give energy to certain things, or you can mark it off in years, but it is most important to let your map flow. If you set things into sections—like, I'm going to achieve this in a year, or that in five years—it can be very troublesome for you.

Then fill the map with the drawings of your needs and wants, placing thoughts in sections to guide you in your quest. When you have drawn all the symbols, you can bead them, if you want, use sequins, or paint them, but set up your drawings as you want them to remain, for this map will become a family heirloom. Your ancient spirit drawing is a doorway of opportunity that will put your needs and wants in order.

3. Reviewing the path map.

On the night that you do this ceremony, date your drawing in the corner and sign your name, making a commitment that one year from that night you will come back, open your map and circle the things that you have achieved. At that time, you will add to the map more drawings of needs and wants that you have put into your spirit journal during the year. You can always add and take away from your needs and wants. Sometimes it's important to learn that you *don't* want something. Then you can remove it from your map by drawing a circle around it and putting a line through it. This shows that you don't wish to achieve this in the twenty-year walk that the ancient spirit drawing will bring forth.

4. One year at a time.

When you sit with this process, it is important to remember that things come to pass from this map. So from the map to the spirit journal, make a 1–25 list of things that you would want to have happen in the next year.

Example: I have forty drawings on my map. I place buying a house, getting an education, and having a child all in one year. I write that on my 1–25, but I realize that maybe that's too much for me to do, so I leave getting an education and having a child on the same page, but put buying a house back into the spirit drawing to wait for a later time. Or maybe I put buying a house in as this year's project and put the other two back in for next year or for some year to come.

After you have gone over your list, make a new list that provides monthly, weekly, and daily goals.

Example: I know I have to work to make money to purchase the land to have a home, so getting a job is on my list for this month.

Sit with your ancient spirit drawings one year at a time, and make out a list of projects each year that you are going to achieve. Break them down into options that you have by being very clear and outlining the steps you need to take. Your map of ancient spirit drawings is your conversation with Great Spirit, Grandmother/Grandfather—you asking and them answering—you opening doors and opportunities coming. Remember, the more you put down, the more you get back.

5. **Closing the map.**
Sign the map, roll it up, tie it, and place it on your altar or within a sacred place. It is not to be opened for another year. Work from your spirit journal where you keep your 1–25s, making lists and carrying out goals and plans, looking forward to circling things and making them come true. At the end of twenty years, your map will be turned into a shield, hung on a round hoop with feathers and other objects that have come to you along the way. Maybe you'll want to attach things like deeds, contracts, and diplomas. Maybe you'll want to frame those things and put them around your map shield. This is a way of celebrating your achievements. You can place your map on the wall, framed in a circle made from wood from the tree people. Place feathers on the map as a reminder. They will act as a voice that will help you learn for the next twenty years. Tie on bands of color that you have worn on your arm (see pages 100–101) to give you confidence.

You will see your life take form through your needs and wants.

It will manifest from the ancient spirit drawings. The choices are yours within this path map. You make them, break them, start with them, finish with them.

The Process of the Lesson of Original

Tools: *Spirit journal and pen; a white candle for spirit; sage or sweet grass for smudging.*

You need to go somewhere that is quiet, where you can think and organize the lessons of Original. Within Original are four lessons.

1. Remember.

Sit and, in your mind's eye, see your life. Make a chronological list of the years that you have lived, remembering the good and the bad. Jot down one or two words.

Example: Worked at the electric company, had child, own six horses.

Put down memories.

Example: Car accident, 1981.

Put down things that you remember, good and bad.

Example: Best friend died in 1973. Went to war.

When you have written down all of your physical two-legged memories, then start to remember things that are spirit.

Example: Spoke with angels, saw elves born. Remember swirling colors, saw dark, brooding, swirling cloud form.

It is important to remember back to Original. When you reach Original, you will see it in bright, white light. You will be at a point of entrance. Step into that light and see. When you step into your memory, go as far back as your mind can see. You will be walking through the corridor of the soul. When you step into the bright, white light, you will be at the point of now. There you will be one with Great Spirit, Grandmother/Grandfather.

2. Feel.

Many times we seek out religion. We want to carry, love, and cherish our spirituality. Look back at your list under "Remember" and write out how you feel about different things. Maybe you've closed doors and don't want to deal with death. Maybe you can't deal with loss. Maybe you are still angry with someone and need to go to them and settle. Take different memories and say how you feel.

> *Example: 1972 my dog died. Many times in my life I have known death. It still feels as uncomfortable as it always has. Now I realize that I have grown past the death of that dog and understand that there is a doorway, for I have accepted and seen the tombstone as a door. I no longer need to grieve for myself, and I can let the dog be free.*

It is important to write down your feelings, to see if you are holding on or letting go. So often we keep anger, discontent, and disenchantment in our lives by simply holding onto our feelings. Work out the feelings by writing them down, or talk them into a recorder. Listen and look at your feelings. Understand them for what they are, neither good nor bad. Just let them flow through your mind or writing.

3. Draw a map of guidance.

Within your life, from your memories, look at the guidance that you have received. Examine your memories for times that spirit has guided you.

> *Example: I heard something. I saw something swish across the floor. I had a feeling when I watched that movie and it spoke to me about ----. I heard God's voice in the rain tonight. It spoke of not being sad when people die.*

You need to draw your guidance map according to the way you hear the voice of Great Spirit, Grandmother/Grandfather. What were the times in your life when God spoke to you?

All guidance may not be helpful. Did you choose to be what you are today, or did someone make you become what you are? Remember, it is never too late to change your career. It is never too late to let go of your anguish and become what you've always wanted to be. You may see within your map that you've been living someone else's life—or that you've been living love. There is no rule in life that says that we have to live for another. We may make a choice to live for others, or choose to give our life away so that others can live. This also might appear in your map of guidance.

A map of guidance will start with childhood in your memories and go all the way to where you are today, with you looking back, making choices. So often we limit ourselves. We must go beyond those limitations.

4. **Write a brief outline of your spirit.**

From your memory and your feelings, briefly examine your spirit.

> *Example: White light, spirit. Blue light, truth. Swirling colors of purple and burgundy, soft peach, and pink. I choose to walk with Truth and spirituality. I see Impeccability, with Balance and spirit. I fear no evil for light is my path. When one brings harm to me, I move aside and move on. As I walk as a human, I will walk in Truth.*

From memories and feelings, guidance and life, comes forth original direction. If yours is a walk of meanness and evil, usage and codependency, it's hard to see these things as light. There are feelings of anger, feelings that have not been put to rest. Walking as a human, it is the spiritual way to go to Original, getting beyond the brooding, and even the foreboding of anger. It is a spiritual thing to walk in the sunlight, to be creative, a creator.

· 6 ·
INNOCENT
COYOTE

I hear the drum, a familiar beat calling us together. I come into the circle within the teaching lodge, and sit on the buffalo robe. I remove my hat and breathe in and out. "Good evening, Grandmother/Grandfather, Great Spirit, and Council of Colors. Give us this opportunity to be a student. Hear us and talk to us. Show us our way within green. Fill our hearts with the teaching of Growth. Help us to learn the lesson of Faith and bring Faith forth as a teaching. Thank you Grandmother/Grandfather. Aho!"

The Talking Stick moves about the room. Different voices share different feelings. What makes you grow? What stops you from growing? Does growing ever stop? How is it that you quit? An interesting topic, with subject matter ranging from being molested as a child to being raped as a young woman, to being told no as a young man, to being raped as a young man. All kinds of topics are discussed around the floor. *I stop me from growing.* This is a statement that some of us have to understand. *I stop me from growing.* I give you your power back—each one of you that sits here this evening, within the presence of the stars. Growth is the doorway that allows your power to come forth. Within growth we must release and let go. Bringing forth Balance as a medicine, bringing forth Creativity to create a space to move on with dignity and honor. I have read in the journals sad, hard, and horrible things that go on. Often we set ourselves up for our own lessons, and they come down the path.

Growth is a fearful place to be. The changing and evolution of change is the mental level of growth. The spiritual level of growth is constant. We are growing on a physical platform. We are remembering spiritually. And to do that, we must release our physical blocks—the holding of old memories. We must let go of the anger that stops our spiritual flow from entering our lives.

The song of the frog fills the room. Each one of us stops to listen to the night breeze underneath the old cedar. The candle lights twinkle in the Rainbow Medicine Wheel. Prayers are hung. The lighting of the green candle is brought forth. We have our Confidence, our Balance, our Creativity, and now our Growth. Each candle is lit in representation of our medicines, releasing, renewal, cleansing. These are the teachings of Growth.

We go to ceremonies from hugging trees to throwing rocks in the river, with thoughts connected to them. The rattlesnake shakes his tail. The Rainbow Snake enters our mind. It comes in through vision and out through reality. Loads are lifted. People's faces lighten as they place the bad memories in a hole and bury them, yell into the depth of that hole and let them go. The lesson of faith is upon us. The green wrist bands are tied next to the yellow. Our arms remind me of Lifesavers. Lifesavers are a reality. Life saving is an opportunity.

Within the rattle we listen to the voice of the Wise Ones. We pray and put our prayers into our ties. We string prayer lines of commitment. A song of honesty is where Growth begins.

These teachings I bring you from the stars. Breathe in and out, and relax. Before us is a very large Grandmother Pine—a huge growth, over four hundred years old. Move towards this large standing one, embrace her and let her embrace you. When you embrace her, give away your feeling of inadequacy and guilt. Give away not being good enough and trying to prove. Put it within her as you hug her and breathe back into

yourself her message. Feel your smallness next to her largeness. See how small your problems are when you are next to her, and let them go. The wind blows through Grandmother Pine and carries our guilt away. The wind swirls and rises and blows harder, blows away our inadequacies. It is done. Forgive. Forget. Dismiss, and let go.

A very small coyote enters the lodge. It shyly walks around and lies at the feet of the raven. It is within each of us to rebirth a new innocence.

List all your angers in your spirit journal and let go. Take in the memory of the small coyote who sits at the feet of magic, for it is a natural opportunity that you have been given, within the teaching lodge, to let go of your regrets, to be at one with your guilt, to stand in new faith, founded in your beliefs. New beliefs are brought forth; innocence is understood. And the green candle flickers in the night.

The lodge empties. A quietness remains. The stars shimmer in the center of the wheel. I sit with the word "guilt." Before me I see a cage. In it I see those held captive within their own minds. A familiar old coyote with a scar over its eye is dancing around the fire, laughing and beckoning, taunting me.

"You have no faith. I'll show it to you. I'll put it in your face and make it real. It's more than being without money. It's more than how to achieve your goals. Faith is more."

The coyote dances. The trickery weaves its web. I shake my head and put on my black hat, remembering that I do not have to look into the cages. I do not have to be afraid for I have opened them tonight. It is with this black hat that I stop abuse. I stand and close the teaching lodge for the night.

I hear the soft sound of the flute calling me back.

Teachings of Spirit—Growth Medicine

The Lesson of Faith

An innocent coyote isn't always what it looks like. A coyote is what it is. The innocence is there until it's tainted, or it's returned once it's lost, by starting anew. This is the process of Growth—an ongoing cycle of letting go and bringing forth. We come from the star people—as star people—to this earth to be two-legged human beings. We are given a beginning of innocence, but as we roll along like a rock in the river, we pick up our story. We're smooth or jagged, depending upon what we interact with. To value our lives, we must understand that growth is a natural cycle. A seed brings forth a blade of grass and then withers and becomes a seed again. Often in our lives we keep things and hold them; we stop the process of flow. We build a wrong, for we have created a dam that blocks energy.

Lessons of Faith are tests of fire. Push yourself to the limit, and then push harder. Then push even harder the next time. Many times we expect more of ourselves than we are capable of giving, and our expectations end in death. Human experience is a very precious thing, as are all things Great Spirit, Grandmother/Grandfather have created. In life it is said that there is evil. Everyone must blame something; the easiest thing to blame is the unknown. The fact is, choice is the thing to blame. You can be lulled into a bad choice by your faith or belief. All is created by

Great Spirit, a Creator, and, as with anything that isn't the way you would wish it to be, it can be changed with choice. If you don't understand this, you make that choice a negative one.

To store innocence is faith. Faith in yourself to begin anew leads to the cycle of growth.

Ceremony of Innocence

The ceremony of innocence is done in the morning just before sunrise, or as the sun rises. It is a ceremony of beginnings, of renewal, and most of all, of awakening.

Tools: *Sacred tools of your choice; cornmeal; sage or sweet grass; a green candle; spirit journal and pen.*

Build a cornmeal circle (page 37), smudge, enter from the East, and make yourself comfortable. Place your green candle in front of you and light it in honor of Growth, of Faith, of Innocence, and Awakening.

1. **Knowing innocence.**
   Write in your spirit journal a clear understanding of what innocence is to you.

   Example: Innocent—fresh, clear, pure, certain.

   After that statement, list the things that change innocence into carnal knowledge.

   Example: Carnal—passion, appetite, flesh, body, sensual, temporary.

   Our innocence is divided in two—spiritual and carnal. To know the difference is the same as right and wrong. To be right is to go with and act in the flow; to be wrong is to hold on, to be stubborn, to block the flow.
   Look within the spirit of each of the words. Look them up in the dictionary. Get a clear understanding of the difference between "innocent" and "carnal," between right and wrong. At what age did you become aware of carnal knowledge? At what age did you learn right and wrong? At what age did you understand innocence?

2. **Release guilt.**
   Looking back over the differences between innocent and carnal,

breathe in and out four times—in through your nose and out through your mouth—and relax. Follow your path to your center, a place where you can think and see. Look at the spirit of innocence and get a clear picture of what innocence is spiritually—the colors, the smells, the objects that represent innocence. Look at carnal and get a sense of what it looks like. Get a clear picture of its spirit. Come back to your reality and understand the difference between human flesh and spirit, light, energy. Understand that, as a human, you are a blend of the two.

Sitting quietly, extend your hands in front of you, palms up to the sky. In your left hand place thoughts of spirit, things of energy, lightness, color, goodness. In your right hand place things of humanness, of flesh, of carnal, things that are heavy, things that die, parts of the self that are separated from the light. Look at the two kinds of things you hold. Be at peace with both sides of yourself. Understand that a blending is necessary.

Release the things of your left hand by letting them go. They'll hover and float. They'll remain constant.

Release the things of your right hand. They'll sink and fall to the ground. They're heavy.

Move your hands back into your lap. Breathe in and out, understanding that you have the ability to release guilt as you breathe. Let go of the depth of guilt, as you understand that humanness is a part of life.

Now list the things that you feel guilty about in your life. When you finish with this list, decide if you wish to carry them any longer. The answer will probably be no. You will want to rid yourself of guilt to become light. The more guilt you get rid of, the lighter you get. Take the paper on which you wrote your list of guilts and burn it, letting it become light. The darkness, the dark pieces will fall to the ground and become ashes. Let them go, and understand that on the earth, things are heavy; they are carnal; they are flesh; they are human. Breathe in and out, and be at peace with the breath, Great Spirit, Grandmother/Grandfather.

3. **Bringing forth, awakening.**

Sitting quietly with the green candle, the flame of Growth, make a list of acceptance, of awakening. The list is to have four parts:

a. Things that take away a part of you (such as negative thoughts—anger, guilt, self-belittlement, fear).

b. Things that inspire you.

c. Things that awaken your happiness.

d. Things that allow you to soar with joy.

Keep this list in your spirit journal, for this is a bringing forth, an awakening of growth that is spiritual.

4. Honoring Growth.

Make a list of things that you can do that represent Growth, that are new beginnings, new awakenings, movements of bringing forth new actions, of starting again.

Example: Start each day with an affirmation that it will be a good day. Look at everything you do as an opportunity to make it into a good day. Look at each thing that is in your life as a good thing, one that gives you an opportunity to have a good day.

In honoring Growth, you will be accepting. Make a list of things you can do to honor Growth.

Example: Plant something; give an opportunity to something; be accepting and open an opportunity to someone; change something and start anew; stop something and start anew.

In honoring Growth, you have the ability to see within spirit, to walk with things in a new light. To have no condemnation, no wrong, no guilt, no lack, brings forth the cycle of Growth. It is a release and an awakening.

Growth Bands
Ceremony of Hair Ties or Wrist Bands

Tools: *Strips of 100 percent cotton cloth cut 1/4 of an inch (.62cm) wide; cotton embroidery thread in the seven rainbow colors; sage or sweet grass.*

Start by smudging all the items you'll be using.

You can cut cloth strips, embroidery thread, colored cord, or yarn long enough to tie around your wrist in the color of the medicine or lesson that you are working with. The wrist band is to be worn as long as the lesson is being learned. I recommend wearing it for a year to attain the fullness of the teaching. During that year, you wear it at all times—in the shower, in the bath, going swimming, having sex, at work, going to the opera, everywhere—being proud of your learning. When you have achieved the lesson by using the medicine and you feel it is solid, remove the wrist band, placing it in ceremony on your lodge pole as a celebration of the lesson becoming a teaching. At any time you feel you have slipped back into the word becoming a lesson, then make a new wrist band and start the process again.

Hair ties are used as a celebration. When you have achieved your lesson, or want to honor a teaching, braid a colored cloth or string into your hair—or, if your hair is too short, tie it around the outside of a lock of hair—to remind you that within the spirit realm you have achieved your teaching. The braid or the lock of hair should be very thin—made of just a few hairs. You wear the hair tie at all times, washing it when you wash your hair, but not removing it. If you choose to wear the braid for a year, you can cut it off at that time and place it on the lodge pole in honor of the teaching. You might consider putting a hair tie on when you first become engaged, or at your wedding, and wearing it for the first year of your marriage—or longer. If you braid it in for your wedding, I recommend that you wear it for at least seven years or for as long as the marriage lasts. The marriage will probably be solid if you manage to keep it in for that long.

It is important to remember that these medicine bands are ceremonial pieces and that you need to run them through the sage smoke four times before putting them on. It honors them to smudge them with the sage smoke and cleanse them in a ceremonial way. Wearing these bands is also a reminder for you to walk in a good way.

The Process of the Lesson of Faith

Tools: *Spirit journal and pen; sage and sweet grass.*

Start by smudging. The lesson of Faith is achieved by learning your belief, learning how to core, learning the fruits of manifestations from spirit, and "walking with tradition." When the lesson of Faith becomes a teaching, you will have a belief; you will know what the core of the belief is; you will walk with the fruits of manifestations of the belief; and you will act upon the belief as a faith.

Faith is always committed to your core philosophy. So if you still have some problems in your philosophy, you will have problems with your faith.

1. **Belief.**

   In your spirit journal list your spiritual belief. Write a paragraph or a page or more about what this spiritual belief is. Look up the word "belief." Get a clear understanding that belief is separate from philosophy, religion, or spirit. It is the concrete coming together of philosophy, religion, and spirituality that forms your belief. State your belief. Write it out. Look at it and see that it is yours, that you're not doing, following, or believing it to make someone proud of you, or because someone else walked with it, but that it is your belief—it's what you find works for you.

2. **Core.**

   a. Describe the foundation of your spiritual belief.

   > *Example: Color is the core picture of Great Spirit. Only color can show the perfect presence of Great Spirit.*

   b. Put core into words of action.

   > *Example: My color is resonating energy. Great Spirit always resonates. Color is vibration moving; Great Spirit is always moving.*

   c. Look for the movement of your core.
      The movement is the first thought you get. Always go with the first thought you have.

   > *Example: Truth is a part of Great Spirit, and truth is blue on the medicine wheel. When you're true blue and loyal, then you are spiritual in a true way. The action of truth is spiritual, a movement of good.*

   d. Understanding core, actions of core.
      When you are clear about the core of your belief, your solidity is at hand.

   > *Example: Have color in your life. See it in all things—the sky, the feelings you have, in all the places in your thoughts. When color is present in your life, Great Spirit is, too. You have joy, happiness, clarity, and fun. If you let anger and*

resentment darken your life, making you full of harm and hate, this is an absence of color, bringing darkness to your life. Being and having color in your life resonates the totality of Great Spirit.

3. **Manifestations of Faith.**

When you get to the core movement within your spiritual belief, you bring forth a number of manifestations. Material manifestations are physical.

Example: Having an education, a career, a house, children.

Spiritual manifestations are fruits.

Example: The value of money, the enlightenment of having children, the endless opportunities of a career, the creativity of a career, the knowledge and insight that education can give you, the essence of home—safety, peace (balance), the essence of spirit (animals, flowers, trees and plants, rocks, water, fire and foods).

List the manifestations of your faith.

Example: Material—education, tradition, and seeing one carry on your ways, bringing forth good times and good feelings in your community. Spiritual—Spiritual understanding, Faith brought forth as a way of seeing life, inspiring a loved one, restoring honor and respect.

When your core spiritual belief is good and clear, full and complete, that solidity will reflect in manifestations.

Example: Education and spiritual understanding. Faith brought forth as a way of seeing life. Tradition and seeing one carry on your ways. Inspiring a loved one. To bring forth good times and good feelings in your community. To restore honor and respect.

If you live to be known for your money or the grandeur of your home, or other material objects, then you *are* those objects. You limit Great Spirit by showing how important to you material and physical things are.

A dark-cored spirit would reflect dark-cored actions, such as rape, stealing, lying, drug abuse, or destruction of the human cycle of life. All darkness is an absence of faith. Faith is a light word. There may be faith in the dark, but it is not true to say that faith is faith in the dark. Faith is a movement of light.

4. **Acting upon.**

When the core of your belief is understood, and your fruits and manifestations come forth, it is an "acting upon." You are acting upon your philosophy. Your life reflects what you believe in. If you have had shabby teachings within your belief, or a broken, dysfunctional family at home, you may see broken fruits and broken manifestations, broken hearts, broken dreams, and a waste of life.

Acting upon faith is hard work, for it is an action of commitment. To be dedicated to having faith *is* faith. Write out in your spirit journal what acting upon means to you.

> *Example: Walking with dedication. Being a seeker. Carrying out organization as a way of life. Knowing yourself to be as you see and know your life to be. Being fair, honest, full of life and fun. Wishing to bring no harm to anyone. Not being mean or bringing ill will to anyone. To walk with growth as a fruit of your labors. To have light as a manifestation of your spirit. To have a core of color, the seven colors of red, yellow, green, blue, purple, burgundy, and to understand the colors as a faith and an eternal belief, which is spiritual belief.*

5. **Walking tradition.**

Your traditions are built from your family, from the flavor that you walk, and the flavor is that of your core and your belief.

> *Example: I honor, above and beyond all, accountability of Confidence, the responsibility of Balance, and the sincerity of creativity. My tradition is to bring an uplifting through Confidence, to demonstrate Patience, to apply Balance, to demonstrate Unity, to be Creative, to bring forth and stand upon Original as its source.*

· 7 ·

RAINBOW WARRIOR

Evening is present. Torches are lit and the gate opens. Students of Rainbow Medicine, seekers of spirituality, come to the medicine wheel in reverence and respect. Their patience is strong. Their unity is their interaction. They are original. Their colors, their clans, are represented. Their faith is needed now, to bring forth loyalty, to learn and be the lesson of Sincerity. Truth will be their medicine tonight and in the weeks to come.

I hear the familiar drum calling us to meeting. We come to the drum when we hear it beat, for there we know will be Wisdom waiting to speak its song to us. I remove my hat and pray. "Grandmother/Grandfather, Great Spirit, thank you for this evening and for these good people. Thank you for the lessons of red, orange, yellow, and green that you have shown us, and for the medicines of blue, purple and burgundy that wait ahead of us, that guide us in the dark even though we do not know it. Dark is just a deep shade of burgundy. Thank you for anticipating tonight the color blue. Grandmother/Grandfather, as we light the candle, we light it in honor of you, for light within blue is you. Aho."

The candles are lit: red, yellow, green, and tonight, blue. We step out on the Ceremony of Loyalty. Before us a whirlwind is spinning. Each one of us looks into the wind. We each see events we know, incidents that each student remembers—overeating to comfort ourselves; drug abuse to mask the pain. The wind is spinning more strongly with every memory. We are in a circle, holding onto our faith, remembering each time, and that with growth comes pain. More memories of pain feed the wind. The pain of being lied to, molested, raped, and so on. Each student lets those feelings loose as the wind picks up speed. I listen for the solo flute, and long to bring it to the room tonight. The harsh wind engulfs all the memories.

And we return to class, the space of now. I pass the talking stick around to hear what feelings each student gave the whirlwind. Each one holds the talking stick and speaks of the blackness of the wind and the darkness of the memories they held. Each of them begins to see the truth, as they turn the bad into good. It isn't until we start to see all as a good thing that we understand the soft spirit of our lives, and truth can resonate in its fullness.

Breathe in and out, and let go. The students become focused and relaxed. Before us we see a familiar path that takes us along the river. There, we are in a spirit world. This river is unlike any on earth. It is a spirit river, and it runs with different-colored water. It is a river that you must cross to find the Rainbow Warrior. We each walk through the river, and, as we do, we look down and see the color that is speaking to us. We remember that color. This color speaks of the bands that we walk with. We step to the other side and there is a pale, pale mist of all seven colors—very pale red and very pale yellow. All the colors are pale—pale blue, pale lavender. We step into that mist, and we are engulfed in color. It shimmers and glistens and fills us full. As we move through the mist, it begins to lighten up. There is a waterfall in front of us and the colors pour down, all seven of them, spilling over the earth, out into the rainbow river. Step behind this waterfall, and as you do, you'll come into a camp-site. We step in and there is the camp, a feeling of home. Pay attention to the surroundings and hold them in your heart.

Ahead, you will begin to see a warrior. This warrior will take on its form for you, and you will see this warrior very clearly. This warrior's identity will be what it wears. It will be the colors that it is wrapped in, the colors that it walks on, the colors that it carries. You will look at this warrior and you will recognize that color, for within there you will see the strong colors of your clan. The warrior will hold out its hand, and it is a color for you. This is your message, this evening, about your truth. It is the medicine you must apply in your life to bring your truth forth, and it is the lesson that you must learn to have your truth. The warrior may give you your message in an object, or may give it to you in just pure color. There may be more than one message. Pay attention to what you see.

The drum beats very rapidly and I call them back.

Remember what you have seen beyond the waterfall, what the Rainbow Warrior has given you. Record it in your spirit journal, for it is important to you.

The evening goes on and the teachings spiral. We share our feelings. Lessons of Arrows that are white. Lessons of Black Horse. Lessons of rushing River Horse. Lessons of Moon Owl and Tree Songs. Lessons of Raven Magic and Big Dancing Sky. It is time that we listen to the teachings of the Rainbow Warrior.

Cover yourself now with your medicine blanket for we will see the spirit of an animal that guides you. It will be your guiding animal. We take a deep breath and the room is filled with the clattering sounds of horse hooves, the cry of the cougar, the howl of the wolf, the flapping of wings, the intensity of the eyes of the deer. There is a breathing, a blending. The Talking Stick goes around, and we tell about the animals we have seen.

"How real it was when I reached out and could see it right in front of me and touch that deer."

"How vivid and clear that eagle was!"

"How powerful the snarl and the teeth of the wolf were when I stared into its face."

The sharing goes on and we hear the feelings of the buffalo, the hummingbird, the squirrels. We hear the different sounds of animals that come, as stories are told within the circle that evening and for nights to come.

You find the truth of your spirit animal in the center of yourself. These are not lessons to be taken lightly. The stories and the teachings that come from the Rainbow Warrior are yours to have in your life any time. Follow the mist and there you will meet with the Rainbow Warrior. Apply the medicine and learn the lessons.

Your spirit story can be shown in a spirit stick. It can be shown in your animal totem. It can be shown in your clan and band colors. You can bring forth the depth of yourself. You can hold it in Clarity in front of yourself and this is your Truth. All of the different visions of Grandmother/Grandfather have been broken out and laid before you. It is a commitment of the blue band that you tie on your arm that brings forth the growth of Truth. It is the commitment of being strong within and knowing what you believe in.

The bear speaks of loyalty within. I look in each student's eyes and see that there is a new knowing of loyalty. Truth is the way of the color blue and bear is its medicine animal. Sincerity is a lesson we draw from the fire. It is the fire medicine. Holding onto the Talking Stick, we speak of the voice of fear and the teachings of the fire. To have and know the lesson of Sincerity, one must be strong with Bear Medicine. We must go within and hear our needs and wants.

The sound of large wings flap overhead. One student is taken back by the wind as the spirit bird passes through the lodge.

We are standing on the threshold of completion. The students have come together with things that were strange to them just a few weeks ago. All the objects on the walls of the teaching lodge mean something now. Everything in life—each tree, rock, bell, or flower—talks to them.

The medicine wheel speaks of dedication and commitment, of being responsible. The lesson of sincerity is theirs. It is from the blue stars that the Truth will come and teach them. Know that, as the bears draw from within to get their food, so will we be loyal to self. It is from commitment, from being dedicated to a spiritual belief, that wholeness will come forth and will be shown by the manifestations of the spirit.

We cover our shoulders with our medicine blankets and keep ourselves warm and centered, safe from the darkness that can come over us. The blanket is filled with medicines. As we rub tobacco, sweet grass, sage, and other herbs into the blanket and become at one with the smell of the fire, we look into each others' spirits, getting a clear vision of each person present in the circle. Our hearts feel a loyal trust.

Breathe in and out, and relax within the loyalty of self, for Truth is in the story of the image of Great Spirit, Grandmother/Grandfather. From spirit resonates energy. From energy comes thought. From thought comes choice. From choice comes matter, and from matter comes image. As we vision by the fire, the teaching of Truth is heard by all present. We each come closer, with Great Spirit's voice.

I see a softness on everyone's face, a blending of their spirit and their physical being. Truths wash away their fears, for fear separates and knocks us off balance. The white light sends forth blue, and it flows as the river, the creek, and the spring babble their stories into our hearts. Flowing is the first step of Sincere. Sincerity moves on and becomes a teaching of Truth.

A quietness comes over the lodge as it empties and the students go their ways. Spirit journals are left for me to read, the sharing of stories. My heart is filled with my loyalty and dedication to my faith. An original process has taken place within me and I am solid within my truth tonight.

I place my black hat firmly on my head. It's a good day to live.

I hear the soft sound of the flute calling me back.

The Lesson of Sincere

Teachings of the spirit that bring about joy, that put our fears in balance, are known as Truth Medicine. Truth medicine is what is so, and sometimes it rips and tears like the teeth of the wolf. The process of the lesson of sincerity is values placed in motion, principles set within our heart. It is from Confidence that we know we can. There is no goal so great that we can't achieve it. The teaching of Truth sometimes separates us from the ones we love. Sometimes it asks us to go on, because we're ready for the next thing. Sometimes it is a bitter, cold voice that closes doors physically as well as emotionally. One can die physically and emotionally in life. To know your soul, you must know Truth. When you live with your truth as an outcome in life, there will be a natural constant flow. You will always be where you need to be. Your lessons will be your life tomorrow. To stand solidly, you place your truth as an action in others' words. You walk your talk. Plans become facts. For you to have, know, and be Truth, understanding is the platform of life—not the understanding of someone else's teaching or expectation, but the understanding of your own spiritual belief.

If you wish to achieve Truth, you must stand with exactness. Many times you will need to separate, and that will be your truth. The Truth is in front of you—as it is—firm and solid. Your truth may sometimes separate you from *the* Truth. There is their truth, and your truth, and *the* Truth. Truth medicine stings; sometimes it supports. Sometimes it is soft and gentle, but the way to spirit is through Truth. When you are ready to bend your knees, to know there is a bigger picture—the spirit world—drop your pride and use it as a breath of life, a teaching. You will not follow false ways, but will be open to total truth for you and be able to explain clearly. This is Truth Medicine, a totality to you on your path.

Spirit Stick

Tools: *A stick, 3 to 6 feet (1–2m) tall, fairly good-sized around; colored cloth; feathers; animal skins; bells; beads; embroidery floss in all seven colors; pieces of sticks and wood—and other natural objects that you may wish to place on your stick; sage or sweet grass.*

A spirit stick will give you a closer and more intimate feeling of your spirit.

Spirit
Stick

1. **Seeing your spirit.**
   To understand what your spirit looks like, smudge and sit in a sacred circle made of cornmeal (page 61). Breathe in and out four times and relax. Before you is a familiar path. Follow it to a quiet clearing. There you will see a pond. When you look into the pond, you will see your spirit. Remember what it looks like, what color it is, what animals may be involved, what shapes. Is it an angel? Is it an animal? Is it a blending of soft purples? When you have your spirit clearly photographed in your mind, bring it back and put it in your spirit journal. Write it all down.

2. **Find your spirit stick.**
   Each stick you find will have its own spirit. Search for the stick that has a similarity to your spirit. The stick can be tall, thick, big, small—anything that reflects your spirit. Color, size, shape, animal connections—all these things can be keys.

3. Decorate your stick.

Apply color or animal skin, feathers, plant parts—anything that relates to your spirit. Wrap the stick with these objects and colors. If you know medicines you need to strengthen your life, apply the color that represents them—red for Confidence, and so on (see page 155). Put bells on to represent the joy of light and to protect your spirit from evil ones and the temptations of life. Tie on pieces of sage and cedar to keep your spirit safe. Animals that represent protection to you in a physical and spiritual way can be added to the stick by tying on their skin or a representation of their skin. You can also use feathers from the winged ones, feathers which have dropped off naturally. This will allow your spirit to soar and be its fullest.

You may want to add a dreamcatcher (page 77) to your spirit stick, to keep dark spirits away, to hold back negative energies, to let only the spirit of light flow through.

4. Placing the stick.

When it is finished, your spirit stick is to be placed in the hallway by your front door. Here it will guard you and protect you from things that you don't want in your home or in your life. Always keep this stick at the front of your lodge—be it a tent, a tepee, or your home. You can carry it with you when you go for walks. It opens the door to those you want to associate with and closes it to those you don't.

Ceremony of Loyalty

Tools: *Cornmeal; rock salt; about 50 sticks, as big around as a pencil or up to the size of your finger, 6 to 12 inches (15 to 30 cm) long; colored yarn in seven colors; a fire pit in the center of your sacred circle, or a white candle to represent Great Spirit, Grandmother/Grandfather; sweet grass or sage; sacred tools of your choice.*

You can perform the ceremony of Loyalty any day, at any time. Build a cornmeal circle (page 37) so that you have a sacred place. When you build this circle, place rock salt within the cornmeal. The rock salt is a symbol of protection. It drives off negative vibrations and does not allow dark spirits to have any interaction with you. It is important, when you are working with this ceremony, to understand that loyalty stimulates protection—that they are interchangeable. Protection and safety are loyalty to your spirit.

If you are performing this ceremony on the ground, do not do it in grass, because the rock salt can kill grass. It is a good idea to do the ceremony indoors, where you can sweep the salt up in a pile and move it away. Or, if you want to stay outdoors, put your medicine blanket on the ground and perform the ceremony on it.

1. Listing memories.

Place your candle in the center of the circle. Honor and pray in respect of Grandmother/Grandfather, and ask for the spirit of loyalty to come into your ceremony. Take the small sticks that you have and think of these age brackets: birth, youth, young adult, adult, mature adult, elder, spirit-ancestor elder. Take one stick for each memory you are working with, and wrap the end with a colored string: red for birth, orange for youth, yellow for young adult, green for adult, blue for mature adult, purple for elder, and burgundy for spirit-ancestor elder. These are sticks of loyalty, sticks of movement. Your loyalty to remaining in the sacred circle of life is the energy within the stick.

As you wrap the red sticks, make a list in your spirit journal of your memories of birth and the youngest period of your life, early childhood.

When you wrap the orange sticks, list memories of your youth—ages seven to eighteen.

When you wrap the sticks in yellow, write of young adulthood from eighteen to thirty.

When you wrap the green sticks, write of adulthood, from thirty to fifty.

When you wrap the blue sticks, write of mature adulthood, from fifty to seventy.

When you wrap the purple sticks, write of the age of the elder, from seventy until Great Spirit calls for you to become spirit.

When you wrap the burgundy sticks, think of what it will mean to be an ascended elder, a spirit guide, the thought that someone hangs onto, the one who pulls them to Great Spirit. Think of what your life will be when you are in the spirit world.

2. Drawing the circle.

Now step outside the circle. If you are outdoors, draw a large circle in the dirt, four feet (1.2m) in diameter. If you are inside, draw a circle on a very large piece of paper or cloth. As you draw it, sprinkle cornmeal, tobacco, and sage to honor the ground. Honor Great Spirit and the sky people, spirits of the earth. Divide the circle into four sections.

3. Placing the sticks.

Look at your spirit journal now, and for every memory that you have from your birth to the age of seven, place a stick in the East section, wrapped in red. Then for each youth memory you have, put in an orange stick, moving towards the South. For every young adult memory, put in a yellow stick, heading towards the South. On through the South, moving into the adult section, put in the green sticks. In the West section of the wheel, heading towards the North, put in the blue sticks. At the North, put in the purple sticks, heading towards the Northeast. At the Northeast, put in the burgundy sticks all the way to the East gate again.

For the ages you have not reached yet, put in one color-wrapped stick in that area, and then put in additional sticks for the times that come ahead of you, so that you will have memories. These sticks are plain; they hold no energy; they do not hold you to the earth, but they allow the door to be opened.

4. Using the Loyalty circle.

This circle is a loyalty to life, a circle to which you can come to do prayers for your age. Here you sit with yourself and think about your walk on this earth. Come to the loyalty circle to think about things that are loyal, to think about ways of staying connected. Sometimes sad times come, and you'll need to come here to recall the happy memories. Every time you remember something from your childhood, from your young adulthood, from your eldership,—every time you think about something you want to be as you get older, you may come and put a stick in this wheel, and think about it. On your birthday, come here and place a stick for a memory of something from the last year.

In your spirit journal, write feelings that you have about being alive. Being physically alive is a loyalty to your spirit. It is loyal to stay on this earth and learn these lessons, no matter how hard they are in life. They are the story of you. As you walk each day, look at these lessons, and share with yourself what you have grown to be. For you have made a commitment to live your life in a good way here in this Ceremony of Loyalty.

If you live in the city or in an apartment, place a special flower box with dirt in your home, and put the sticks there.

Let the sun and the moon come across this ceremony and keep this circle up. If the sticks get knocked over, put them back in place. You need to arrange with someone to take this ceremony down after your death, and to burn the sticks to set your spirit free. The burning of the sticks is to be entrusted to a close loved one, and the ceremony itself is to be part of your funeral. After the end of your earth walk, your spirit is free from its loyalty to being a human.

These are the lessons of the Ceremony of Loyalty—being connected in a physical and emotional way, to the spirit.

The Process of the Lesson of Sincere

Tools: *Sacred tools of your choice; white candle to represent Great Spirit; four blue candles to represent the directions of the lesson of Sincere; cornmeal; sage or sweet grass; spirit journal and pen.*

Go to a sacred circle, or build one from cornmeal (page 61), starting in the East. Smudge and enter the circle from the East, taking your spirit journal and pen with you.

1. **Feelings.**
   Breathe in and out four times. Find a soft breath and continue breathing. Before you is a sacred path. Follow this path and you will see a place in your mind's eye, a place of quiet, a center of tranquility. Sit there and you will begin to feel. It is important to feel the spirit, to allow the spirit to feel. In this place of sacred quietness, you will see the sun, and you will feel the spirit sun. You will remember this feeling and the colors that you feel. You will begin to see these colors all around you—very soft, pastel colors. You will feel them and you will feel what they remind you of. What they are saying to you is what you remember.

   You will come back to your physicality and record your feelings in your spirit journal. Record the feelings of the path, the feelings of the tranquility center, the feelings of the spirit sun, and the spirit colors. Record them so you know their feeling.

2. Knowing.

Sit or lie very still and relax. Breathe in and out. In your mind's eye, follow the path that is very familiar to you. Go to a place that is the tranquility center. When you come to this place of tranquility and peace, sit there. You will have the knowledge that you are not alone. You will feel the presence of an animal spirit. Your knowing will look in its direction, and there will be an animal, and you will know its kind. You will know what it is telling you, what it says to you, what it means to you. You may sense other animals as well, and know what they are, where they are, and what they have come for. You will have a knowing that they bring to your mind.

Come back to your reality, and write this in your spirit journal. Record the animal or animals that you have seen and what they have come for.

Example: I sit in my tranquility center and see a squirrel playing by a tree. I know that it is autumn, a time to gather, to prepare for the darkness of the winter. The squirrel tells me that I am always to be in balance, prepared for tomorrow. I know that it is a good thing to use and keep at the same time.

3. Carrying.

Sit in your circle and think about your feelings, the colors that you saw, the way the sun felt, the animals that have come to you. Write in your spirit journal the things that you will need to carry these medicines.

Example: I would like to have some acorns. I would like to have a bandanna that is soft peach. I would like to gather some leaves of autumn, some berries and some nuts. I would like to put some squirrel hair in the bandanna. I would like to build a bundle of sincerity. My sincerity is in knowing my balance for the winter months, not eating too much nor eating too little, but putting away, as the squirrel does, so I will be ready for the winter. I will build my sacred bundle of Sincere, for I am sincere about taking care of myself as a squirrel takes care of itself in the winter.

When you build a bundle of Sincere, a sincere bundle, it is

reminding you to be in balance; it is reminding you to be creative; it is reminding you to grow from the teachings of the bundle. A bundle of Sincere is the best way to walk with the lesson itself, because, having it, you know that each day you are living what you believe.

Go and build a bundle from what you have seen, from your feelings and from your knowing. Place it on your altar, or underneath your bed, or at the foot of your bed. You will go to this bundle once every day and make prayers with the bundle that you will do things in a good way. For it is within Sincere that you learn the truth of life, that you see the loyalties, that you must take care of yourself, and honor yourself.

4. Caring for.

Sit with your spirit journal and ask yourself what gifts have you received from feelings? What gifts have you received from knowing? What gifts have you received from carrying? Think of things that you carry with you, and make a list of them. Think of things that you carry around in your home, and make a list of the special things that you have. Ask yourself why you carry these things. Take time to sit with your objects. Take time to sit with your loved ones in your mind now. Make lists of things that you carry.

> *Example: I have golf clubs, a bike, a big shaggy sheep dog, and a parakeet. See these as bundles of Sincere, that you are the keeper of these bundles. Maybe you haven't played with the golf clubs, or you haven't ridden the bicycle, or played with the animal, or you haven't taken good care of it.*

Look at these things from the eyes of Sincere, and understand that it is very important to care for what you carry. It is a sincere thing, when you have something, to take care of it. If you are not going to take care of these things in the way of a sincere bundle, then let them go. Put them up for sale, give them away, turn them loose. Take care of what you have, for it is Sincere.

When you are insincere, you bring bad medicine into your life — you lose things, things are forsaken. Take care what you carry. It is yours.

· 8 ·

PRAYER MESA, THE ALTAR

I breathe in and out, carefully, relaxing. Four breaths. Before me I see a path. I go where it leads. I sit with the elders, the ancestor elders, the color council. The council of spirits comes together around me. They are grandfathers and grandmothers. Their quietness is rich and full. The council sits together—spirits, shapes of flame, a shifting of color in each one—from pale to bright, soft to strong. I am asked to sit with this council by an elder, a wise old woman cloaked in dark, rich green. "The Grandmother of Faith," she says, soft words whispered on her lips. "I am the Grandmother of Faith."

She motions for me to join the council. As I sit with the spirits, I look to the North and see a mesa, an altar. There are candles glowing all around the edge, little bowls of flame, different colored spirits in bowls. As I look closer, I see they are stars expanding light around the mesa.

Stories begin to go clockwise around the circle, as the different spirits speak. One spirit stands and says, "I am the Moon Spirit." I see the shimmering, soft blue, silver, and purple of her hair. It is the spirit of Woman. She speaks about the richness of being woman, about the softness of nurture, about the kindness of giving within Clarity. She speaks of Wisdom. She sits.

Another grand spirit stands. This one is the Sun Spirit—Sun Man. He speaks of age, and he speaks of Wisdom. He speaks of the talents that flow from the river, from the fire that burns within that speaks Truth. He joins the circle again.

The different spirits stand in all their colors from red to burgundy. The council of stars speak. They talk about earning Confidence, of having Patience. They talk about having Unity and being Balanced. They talk about doing what is right, for the Great Spirit watches.

One star, Burgundy, speaks strongly about Impeccability. "It is hard for the two-legged on earth to remember Loyalty. It is hard to learn the lessons of Reason and always have answers. But with Patience, as time goes on, all things are seen for what they are. You must remember that within Impeccability your word is your strongest bond. It is the thing you need to do the most, the thing you need to organize and stand on. It is from the word that all things come forth. It is from the Impeccable way that you achieve the purpose you know you have. We must work hard. Hard work is within Impeccability." The spirit sits down quickly, and color swirls around the circle.

The Burgundy passes me with a silver flash, and I sit in the quietness. An old woman rises and begins to speak of prayer. The Prayer Mesa— the altar—is set in the teaching lodge. Evening has begun and the two-legged students come down the road. They have the red, orange, yellow, green, and blue teachings now. They have been here awhile, and they think they know things. They go to the Rainbow Medicine Wheel; they honor and place sage. They put down cedar bundles. They do their prayers; they hang them on the lines. My assistant stands with a sternness in her face and beats the drum, calling the students to come to the prayer mesa.

We are here, within this ceremony, in a dark room filled with small bowls of twinkling light. Tools are laid out on the altar, the mesa, the place of prayer. Students come, and when they are called by name, they sit and listen to the spirits speak. There is talk of the objects on the mesa. There are prayer sticks, spirit sticks, talking sticks, bowls of cornmeal to feed the spirits.

Ancient wisdom has come together in this place. The teachings of Wisdom are within the prayers. You can take a run at it one way, and you can take a run at it another; you can run around in a maze like a mouse. Then you can come and you can do it in a good way.

Prayer Mesa

You come to the mesa to listen, to pray, to be given your vision of wholeness. As the students comes to the mesa and do a prayer, they receive a vision of wholeness and hold it in their mind. They are waiting in silence for the whispered sound of their spirit names to come forth, for the shaman is a name-giver. It is up to me, the shaman, to give them their names. I see their eyes. I see them anticipating an animal name — the name of a great eagle. One, who is given the name of the elements, makes the remark, "I always wanted an animal name." The lessons of Wisdom, are hard to learn. You are given the name that you walk with in your spirit, for your name is your spirit. There are names such as "One Who Stands With Clenched Fist," "Running Deer," "Singing Trees," "Whistling Brooks," "Soft Wind," "Black Horse," "Black Wolf," "Yellow Eyes." All names are the same. All names are sacred.

The voice is that of prayer. We pray for your name, for your inner spirit to come forth. There you will hold within you the name. You might be a Dream Keeper, one who holds dreams. You might be a Rainbow Maker, one who organizes dreams, holding on for all they are worth, carrying them to the altar each day and leaving them there with prayers. All of us hold names within us. They come forth in the circle of whispering. The sacred name ceremony awaits those in the Crossover. They have come for their names.

At the prayer mesa there is respect for the stars. They listen and hear what the stars have to say. It is when you have learned the lessons of Patience, Unity, Original, Faith, Sincere, Reason and Worth, that you can walk in a good way—that you understand that every day these lessons will come to you from your spirit. To have the lesson of Worth within the spirit is to know your depth, to know how to keep going and to bring these things forth in your wholeness. It is with pride that you walk with these things, holding onto the lessons. It is yours to pull away and give up, and it is yours to keep walking and not give up.

The ceremony of Crossover begins. It is a time of celebration, for you have crossed over from the things that you do that tempt you away from wholeness. When you have these red, orange, yellow, green, blue, purple, and burgundy bands on your wrists, you are the one who keeps your spirit. You need to be the spirit keeper for your physical self. Your self walks as a two-legged on this earth mother, and you must be the keeper of that spirit. You must remember to nurture it, feed it, play with it, to let it play. Listen to it; let it guide and teach. The ceremony of Crossover is where you share your wholeness. It is a place where you come together in a physical way and prepare to cross over in a spiritual way. For someday, when the road darkens, and you drop your physical robe and die a physical death, you will cross over the Rainbow Bridge and there the spirit horse will wait for you and carry you home. These ways are ahead for all of us, whether we are Protestant, Jewish, Catholic, black or white, Native or yellow. The ways of death lie ahead of us. Then our spirit goes across that bridge into the spirit world, and on.

The students wait, anticipating the joy of Crossover, waiting for the Burgundy lesson to come forth, understanding the power within Impeccability. I watch them gather their things, place their spirit journals. I tell each of them to be in a quiet space, to do as much silence as they can between now and the ceremony, and to watch carefully what they see, as they wait to hear their spirit name and connect with their spirit self.

A quietness comes to the Lodge. My breathing is easy and soft. I sit motionless on the buffalo robe. A very soft spirit dances around the circle. I watch its shimmering ways. I follow it down a path, a path that leads me through a canyon. I come to the same quiet circle where the council has been. I see prayer lines where prayers have been made. I sit with the prayers. I hold a flute in my hand, and I play the song of the night. The song of the prayer mesa echoes around the walls of the canyon. I look beyond the fire—the Black Horse stands, a familiar smile, a familiar look in its eye. It is a friend, a dear friend. A fullness fills our hearts; we know that we have walked the way. I turn and there is the Grey Wolf. I see that strong pride in the wolf's eyes. For knowing how to lead others to the Rainbow Path is the heart that Grey Wolf walks with.

I look the other way and there stands the River Horse, with an intensity of dedication, a celebration of hard work. River Horse is coming forth to her dedication of walking as a good student. I know that the students want to share the Good Red Road. The spirits tell me in their strength that we have walked in a good way, and they have found their paths. Many star people are here, speaking their truths beyond the mesa. Many more two-leggeds are coming. I see them walking with their sadness and their broken hearts, with their religions that do not work and are dead, with their financial systems and dreams and schemes that are gone to old age. I see them come. They remind me of the one who rides the bull: it's only eight seconds, but it seems like eternity. I see them where they have fallen and gotten back up. Or have they been on the wagon and fallen off? They have had to start over again, sell everything and build from the ground up. They have gone as low as they can go. I see their heads hanging. I throw my hat in the air. I raise my hands with pride, and I sing the Song of Wisdom. "It is to be wise," the star people say. "We are to have Wisdom." And the wind blows through the cedar trees.

The evening has turned to late night. The candles, I put them out. Red. Orange. Yellow. Green. Blue. Purple. And next week, we will light that one, the one we are looking for, the Burgundy one. We will stand in the spirit of the river and hear the heartbeat of home.

I hear the soft sound of the flute calling me back.

Teachings of Spirit—Wisdom Medicine

The Lesson of Reason

Within the purple star, Wisdom comes forth as a medicine. Wisdom is the lady who opens the door, the lady of the Way. The soft, feminine energy of Wisdom is our eternal strength. Wisdom Medicine comes from ancient teachings, sacred spirit drawings, voices of your animal guides, knowing your clan. It is not just within the Native American heritage that there are clans. When I speak of the clan, I speak of all people, for all people come to the color. Before there were people, there was color. Color became words. And words became people.

Wisdom gives me a knowing of the realms, of the dimensions, of the realities. It is Wisdom to know that the lessons must be teachings and will be taught. And when they are, they have their Worth. It is a wise thing to know Reason. It is a wise thing to operate from the Original, which takes you to the core. The core is the song of the spirit and the spirit is in the stars and beyond.

Ceremony of Prayer

Tools: *Cornmeal; a piece of cloth; 40 prayer ties (page 34); white and purple candles in holders; a bowl of water; a bowl of dirt; a feather; prayer sticks; spirit sticks; talking sticks; spirit soul dolls and any other sacred tools you wish; sage or sweet grass for smudging.*

Prayer is an easy thing. It is communication between you and Great Spirit, done in your mind, brought forth with words. During this ceremony you will bring forth a prayer mesa, an altar, a place where you will go to do your prayer ceremony. Your prayer mesa should be built in a quiet place. Smudge. Make a cornmeal circle (page 37), and at the top of the circle, when you are facing it, lay down your cloth and that will the North. If you wish, put it in the North direction exactly, or you can designate a spot as North. The cloth can be 100 percent red cotton, or a woven rug, or a 100 percent cotton colored towel—your choice. You may use your favorite color, or the color of your clan or band, or a color that you walk with in a lodge or church. Where you place your cloth will be your altar. Place on that cloth, in the center, a lit white candle that represents Great Spirit, Grandmother/Grandfather. Then, at the top, you place a bowl of water, a bowl of dirt, a feather, and a purple candle, which is lit from the center candle and brings forth Wisdom.

On the cloth lay other objects, things that bring you to concentration—focal points—things that allow you to listen and be in communication with Great Spirit, Grandmother/Grandfather. You can place prayer sticks, rosaries, crosses, any objects of spiritual value. All beliefs are welcome. All religions are welcome at a prayer mesa.

The ceremony of prayer is to be done in your time of need. It may be performed at any time of the day, as many times a day as you wish. Prepare for the ceremony of prayer by making 40 prayer ties in purple to take to your prayer mesa, to balance you and prepare you to be creative in bringing forth your prayers.

1. Opening address.

The ceremony of prayer always has an opening. It is an honoring, an acknowledging of all that is. It is performed by raising your head to the sky and extending your arms above your head to honor and embrace Great Spirit, the voice from within, the soul.

Then extend your arms down to the earth. Honor, receive, and respect the spirit of the Earth, for it is a voice of Great Spirit, Grandmother/Grandfather.

Bring your right hand over to your left shoulder, and then put it out in front of you with the palm up. Move it across your body and extend it all the way out to the right side of your body. This honors the teachings of the colors, the vibrations, the sound, the face of Great Spirit, Grandmother/Grandfather.

Then close your hand in a fist, bring it back, place it on your heart, and breathe in and out four times. Continue breathing and address Great Spirit, Grandmother/Grandfather by title.

Example: "*Aho, Great Spirit, Grandmother/Grandfather, Creator. I make these prayers in Christ's name.*"

2. The acceptance for Great Spirit, Grandmother/Grandfather.

After the opening has been exchanged, it is time to show acceptance for Great Spirit, Grandmother/Grandfather, Creator.

Example: "*I believe and acknowledge Your power Great Spirit, Grandmother/Grandfather. I know You to be the creator of all, light and dark. I know You hear at a time of suffering and sorrow. I know You to be there when I need a good friend. I am in full acceptance of You and am a servant, a child of Yours, a star, Great Spirit, Grandmother, Grandfather, Creator.*"

3. The question, needs and wants, general conversation.

After you have opened and addressed Great Spirit and acknowledged an acceptance, it is time for communication. Pray as if you were talking to a good friend,—using ordinary speech. And then be sure to listen. There will be a feeling of words exchanged between you and Great Spirit, Grandmother/Grandfather. You can ask in the form of questions; you can talk about needs and wants; you can take your trials, tribulations, and worries before the Great Spirit, Grandmother/Grandfather, Creator. It is never appropriate to pray for harm to come to others, for that is not the way of Great Spirit. You can bring forth answers, but remember that Great Spirit never tells us to be selfish or to persecute others, and will never give us the right to take vengeance upon anyone or to take a life.

Great Spirit, Grandmother/Grandfather is where you bring your heart's desires, where you can ask to be forgiven and to forgive others.

Example: "Great Spirit, I ask for Your forgiveness for I may have forgotten You yesterday. I may have been too busy living the worldly life to remember to sit down and speak to you, Grandmother/Grandfather. I am truly sorry for this, for sometimes I am weak and I forget to pray. Forgive me."

4. Go forth and act. Closing.

It is important to know that you have listened and felt the presence of Great Spirit at the prayer mesa. You need to know that you can feel the Holy Spirit, understand that you are guided by it, and receive answers strongly within yourself.

In closing a prayer, it is always a good thing to say thank you. "Thank you, for it's a good day to live. Thank you, for it's a good day. Thank you, for it's a good day to die." Another closing that might be appropriate is, "I pray this prayer in Christ's name, Aho." It is not the purpose of the prayer mesa to become religious, but we are all one race and all religions come together in the circle of Rainbow Medicine, which was at one time a band of colors, and will be again.

Through the closing, you give thanks and receive the blessings and the will of Great Spirit, Grandmother/Grandfather.

Example: I go forth now as I have listened to my prayers and heard you speak to me, Great Spirit, Grandmother/Grandfather. You have guided me in your elegance. I will go forth and live the light that you have shown me. Thank you for the blessings that you have bestowed upon me. I pray this prayer in the memory in honor of the circle and of the eagle. Aho.

The Prayer Mesa Stick

Tools: *Two sticks 10 to 18 inches (25 to 45cm) long; threads in seven colors; seven colors of paint; bells; moss; cedar; strips of blue cloth 1/4 inch (.6cm) wide; glue; sage or sweet grass.*

The mesa stick, when in place in the ground, can take the place of an entire altar. This allows you to travel and still be able to set an altar wherever you wish. It is a point of focus that is also interchangeable with the center of the medicine wheel (Great Spirit), so you can carry the complete medicine wheel with you, as well.

The mesa stick may be left as a guard over the area where you have been working, keeping the space sacred. When you're finished with the ceremony, leave the stick, and disconnect physically from it totally, letting the wind and other elements remove its presence over time. Meanwhile, you can reconnect to the physical place through your spirit. All you have to do is think of the space where the stick is physically, and your spirit can travel back to it in your mind and continue its work whenever you want. If a loved one were sick, for example, and you could not be with them, you could leave the mesa stick in their presence, and explain that you are with them in prayer. This allows your spirit to connect, and they are never alone.

Start by smudging all the articles you will be using. A prayer mesa stick is made of two sticks tied together—one male and one female. You will find one stick that represents the female, which is the moon stick, and another that represents the male, which is the sun stick. Make sure that the moon stick is a lighter color than the sun stick.

Prayer Mesa Stick

1. Wrap the sun stick in moss and cedar to represent the private area of a male. Wrap colored threads that speak of the male energy (red, orange, and yellow) around the top of the stick.

2. On the female stick put a strip of blue cloth to represent the female parts of the woman. Paint in blue the face of a woman on the stick. Keep the face simple by painting two round circles for eyes, one round circle for the mouth.

3. Dress both sticks in appropriate things adding on bells, stars, moons, and beads, or painting the sticks with appropriate symbols (sun, moon, stars). Wrap the bottom of the female stick with threads of appropriate colors for the female: green, blue, purple, and burgundy.

4. Connect the sticks at the center with a belt of wholeness. This is done by braiding or binding together the sticks one over the other and tying them in the center with seven colors of thread. Paint purple dots on the bottom of each stick to represent wholeness.

The Process of the Lesson of Reason

Tools: *Any sacred objects; medicine blanket; cornmeal; white and purple candles; spirit journal and pen; sage or sweet grass.*

Go to a quiet place, build a cornmeal circle (page 37), smudge, and step in from the East with your medicine blanket, spirit journal and pen. The process of the lesson of Reason is to answer your questions. It is to rid you of blame and help you to own situations for what they are.

1. **Honor.**
   Make a list of things that have brought you honor in your life. Then make a list of things that have brought you dishonor. Look at the situations of dishonor and see them as choices that you now have. Understand that no matter how much disrespect you have brought to yourself, there were reasons—and the choice is now yours. Look back through the situations of dishonor in your life, and write out what you would do if you could do it over.
   When you have listed all the things of dishonor, tie twenty purple prayer ties and offer a prayer of forgiveness for yourself, along with

a prayer of support from Great Spirit, Grandmother/Grandfather, and a prayer of thanks for showing you the reasons.

2. Purpose.

Write the purpose of your existence in your spirit journal. List reasons why you feel you came to this earth. List reasons why you have the right to persecute, or to be selfish, or to bring pain upon others. Connect yourself to a color that brings evil to others. No, you can't do it. There is no color within the bands of the clans of color that brings about evil. Sometimes people place blame on red or black, but red is the color of Confidence and black is the color of wholeness—neither are colors of evil. Evil has no color. It is not transparent, it is not clear. It does not exist within the bands of Great Spirit, Grandmother/Grandfather.

Colors stand for purpose, the purpose of honor and respect, of sacred. If anger seems to be within your purpose, work it through with prayers for the things that bring anger to you. Anything you have listed within your purpose that is evil or negative may be brought to prayer through prayer ties within purple for Wisdom to overcome. Your purpose sets forth a pattern of wholeness for you to follow. There should be solidity in your purpose, which is your character, your drive, your dreams, and your vision.

Sit within the circle and bring to yourself acceptance of spirit. Think of Great Spirit, Grandmother/Grandfather, and form a clear picture of your purpose, of how you are connected to it. Accept what is good and what is right. Keep it personal to yourself, separate from other people, as a private thing.

3. Flow.

The flow of Great Spirit, Grandmother/Grandfather is the purpose of Reason. List in your spirit journal the things that get you into the flow. Write down the places where you flow.

Example: singing, playing music, teaching children, writing, going to work, playing with animals.

If you are blocked in this area, there is a reason and you need to go to the core. Go deep within flow and identify what is blocking you. What are you angry at? Whom do you wish harm to and why? How have you become separated and what caused it? When you go to the core, you can look at your inadequacies. When you get to the core of a feeling, go even deeper. Who did I dislike before this person? What was it that happened to me at an even younger age that caused me to be this angry? When you reconstruct your flow, it's important to understand that your anger started at an early age.

And layers of anger lie on top of each other, one after another, until you have created hate. Hate is a stagnation of energy. It stifles and destroys. Instead of moving forth and creating, you are blocked and stopped. Flow is a simple understanding of truth versus lies. It's an acceptance of Great Spirit, Grandmother/Grandfather in a good way.

4. Actions.

To bring forth actions of Reason, you need Clarity. There must be honor and flow within Reason for it to be a teaching. This brings a wholeness to purpose.

List the actions of Reason. Also list your blocks and hatreds.

Example: Actions of reason — Joy, happiness, fulfillment, wholeness, bravery. Blocks: harbored anger, resentment, jealousy, and greed.

Understand these feelings. Take responsibility for yourself and stop blaming others. Get on with the flow. Then you can go forth and do something in your life. Life is full of art, music, sports. It's full of bringing forth contentment and peace. It need not be a place of war, rape, and murder. It need not be people who are out of control — who have lost their honor, who have been disconnected from their peace, their purpose, their flow — whose actions bring forth dark and evil ways. But that is their choice. By choice they do not understand the reasons — that underneath the anger is fear, and that fear acts out in a way that controls: a fear of being alone, a fear of being separated from, a fear of not being good enough.

List your fears, look at them, and take them through the process of coring, going within the center to see what is there. Then, when you look at the important things in life that bring fear and worry, like school, work, family problems, children, and wrong actions, understand that those things are opportunities — opportunities to have purpose. Remember not to confuse purpose with an addiction or bad habit. A purpose sets direction for your life; it brings Clarity, happiness and joy.

Within actions you bring forth your purpose. Take responsibility for what you do, understanding that accountability and responsibility bring about Sincere. Sincerity puts you in balance and brings forth the teachings of Reason.

List the wild things you do and the tame things you do. Look at the purpose of the wild things, and look at the purpose of the tame things. Bring about the reasons behind the walk of yourself. After you make a list of both things, write a statement of what each mean to you. See the purpose and understand the purpose of the wild side of yourself and then the purpose of the self. You are in charge of your purpose.

· 9 ·

SACRED HEART

It is dark in the teaching lodge. I enter this week alone. It is a week that is spent in quiet in the students' lives, one in which they prepare themselves to cross over. The Crossover celebration is a time in which they will be acknowledging their presence in the earthly plane and in the spirit world. It is a time when they will be held accountable for their spiritual knowledge. It is also a celebration in which they become a part of the medicine wheel, the ones who know Great Spirit, Grandmother/Grandfather, Creator. They will be celebrating their personal religion and belief.

I light the burgundy candle in the darkness. Sitting here on my buffalo robe, in the quietness of the night, I am in the sacred heart of Truth, of spirituality, of existence. I breathe easily and slowly and beat a heartbeat on my drum that carries my spirit. I circle through the lives of each student in my mind. My spirit reaches out and touches them. I smile in their life, for I am proud that they have taken time to listen to Great Spirit, Grandmother/Grandfather, to acknowledge the spirit side of themselves. As I beat gently on the drum, I feel honored to carry with me Impeccable Medicine. My memories of Grandmother/Grandfather Wolf and Impeccability are all around me. The spirits of the colors dance in the room. Star people dance around me. They leap with joy.

A blue star stops and looks me in the eye. "This is good work you do, Wolf Moondance. You enable them to feel good about their spirit. Truth resonates when they feel good. There is a sincerity that becomes solid in their lives when good is their path. Come with me tonight. Come past the heart. Come past the mind. Go through the soul, the corridor of life. Dance with me in the realm of beyond. Come with me, Wolf Moondance, and begin the Crossover."

I hold hands with the star, and we walk beyond, into the realm of spirit and beyond that. I pass through the plains, and the wind spirals around me. I feel a pull towards home. I am there, within this grand burgundy light. It is all burgundy around me. It looks black, deep black. There is a pulsating beat and a resonance of spirit. I feel as if everything is me, and I am everything.

I look in front, and there are eyes. I turn in a circle all the way around me, and with each movement, I see a thickness of colored eyes. They look dark, deep-set. I step on through these dark eyes, and the sense of foreboding becomes familiar—the eyes are burgundy now. Then I realize that the eyes are actually points of light that only look like eyes. These points of light are burgundy. Walking on, they are purple. Walking on, they are blue. Walking on, they are green. Walking on, they are yellow— yellow eyes as deep and as wide as can be. Walking on, they are orange. Then they are red.

There is a knowing now, for I am no longer as you would know me in bodily form. There is a knowing in this energy that I have. It is a spiral moving backwards that I follow. Sitting now, in a quiet mist, in vibrant white, I remember. Silver stars glisten, all points of the brightest white light spiral around me, dancing, rejoicing, and singing. Spinning in a clockwise motion, a whiteness is all—with sparks of color and softness all around me. It is eternal, endless, forever, this way. We are beyond before. We are and always will be in Great Spirit, constant, infinite, always. Color shimmers and sparkles. All is. A movement of spirit emerges—a shadowing spirit lurks. Will has developed and choice is. Words of grandness and sparks fly. Counterclockwise spins out—clockwise spins in. The spiral begins falling. Upwards remains and downwards becomes. Blue expands into black and spirals downwards. I watch it descend.

Stars cascade downwards, following Will, and become Choice. A completion emerges. Totality exists—before and after—dismiss and hang on. Opposite has emerged. I find myself sitting quietly in the world of angels and spirits. I watch them dance. I watch them worship. I am apart, as I watch.

In front of me stands a spirit of integrity, of a grand mystery, a spirit of Impeccability. It turns its head to the left and looks. Its face is a star and a half circle. Its body is light, shaped as a human. Its feet are long and thin. It is wrapped in shades of burgundy, a sweep of color that looks like cloth. Its hands are long and narrow, with stars on the ends of the fingers. Around its head spiral burgundy rays, with bands of shimmering stars in pastel colors. Its eyes are infinite, soft, and beautiful. It is an angelic form—beyond anything I have experienced. Radiating from it is golden light and silver light, and every time it steps, the stars bounce.

"Hello," I say.

"Hello." "Hello." "Hello." "Hello." A voice echoes from the being. Four hellos. I feel them touch me, embrace me, encompass me. I feel

heart—not a muscle that beats and pounds, but heart that knows warmth, compassion, sincerity.

"It is good to see you," spirit says. "It is good that you can remember. It is for all to remember. It has been very long since anyone remembered the ones who turned their back on eight." Spirit smiles. "Remember for a moment."

My spirit knows that a circle is an eight—four directions, four points where the directions are born.

"There is no beginning in an eight. It is a constant movement of clockwise and counterclockwise. There is no division known as evil and good—only in the human's experience. This is the curse. When evil is endured and brought forth as a way of life, the movements separate and half becomes a counterclockwise circle, shutting both hearts off to life. They closed their door to what lies ahead, what lies beyond Earth, what lies beyond the celestial, what is here beyond the spirit world. Life is simply a mystery to those who shut their hearts down. It is a time of expansion and opportunity to reunite those movements, that choice, the eight. To walk in the circle both forwards and backwards. And to feel the presence of honor and respect."

These words the spirit of Impeccability speaks clearly in my heart. I take a deep breath and look at the height of this spirit. It is so tall, so vast.

"That's right. Within Impeccability there is no limit. It is forever, absolute. The correctness is understanding," the Spirit smiles.

"I know, Spirit. It saddens me. It saddens me to be a human. I listen to us talk every day about why did we have to come to such a pitiful place? Why do we have to endure death?"

Laughter rings out through the spirit world, and a bright silver flash streaks from the spirit's eyes. It shoots out around me and seems to lighten forever—not for moments as we know lightning, but forever as light really is. The silver flash lights up everything around me, and the fullness glimmers with color.

"Would they want to live forever in that mess—in the split of eight? Dark are the memories you walk with. Choice is a two-sided thought, one of right, one of wrong. Why would anyone want to limit themselves? It is within knowing and peace of mind and sacred heart that one might find what one seeks. It is good that you have come, that you have taken a moment to look at the face of Impeccability. Strive for the eight—two sets of four, black and white."

The words dance around me and I am in constant.

Then the sun sets. It is dark. I am again sitting in my teaching lodge, looking at Impeccability, thinking of Impeccable as Absolute—thinking of Impeccable as correct, ideal, perfect, clear, pure. I watch the flame dance on the burgundy candle. I move backwards in lighting the colors. I light purple, blue, green, yellow, orange, red. As I watch the colors go backwards, I unwind my mind. I look at the things that were bad in my life, and I see the good that was standing just to the side of them. Thoughts go backwards. I reach the burgundy and blow the candles out: red, orange, yellow, green, blue, purple. My thoughts run forward, thinking of all the good things that have happened, all the joy and laughter, all the fun—all the really big, good times. I feel my heart beyond sacred. It is rich and full.

I roll myself up in my buffalo robe, and go into the night as the burgundy flame dances.

I hear the soft sound of the flute calling me back.

Teachings of Spirit—Impeccability Medicine

The Lesson of Worth

Impeccability is actions brought forth from spirit. Understanding Impeccability is knowing you are connected to your spirit. Four thoughts are the teachings of impeccability. *Don't. Do. Is. Not.* Within this circle of *is, do, don't, not,* you have the movement of positive and negative. It is only in human life that we are limited to *don't* and *not.* Beyond human existence is the realm of *is* and *do.* When we draw from our spirit, when we live with our spirit, we are in the Will of Great Spirit. The Will of Great Spirit is Impeccability for it is *do* and *is.* There is no *not* or *don't* within Impeccability. So within the teachings of Impeccability, I must remind you to be careful, for you have the duality of the conditional and the unconditional. It is very, very hard to be unconditional within human bounds, for within the Earth and on the Earth and amongst the Earth there are limitations of greed, selfishness, and jealousy. There is inadequacy and limitation. These things are to be respected and understood as the lessons that you endure each day. It is through Impeccability that you can pass beyond unconditional in your life as a human, for in human life condition is unconditional, and unconditional is conditioned. These things get turned around. Think about it. Live with it. You'll get it. For these are the teachings of Impeccability.

Ceremony of Impeccability

Tools: *Cornmeal; sage or sweet grass; spirit journal and pen; seven candles in holders: red, orange, yellow, green, blue, purple, burgundy, and matches; or seven colored sticks as big around as your thumb and seven inches (18 cm) long. If you use sticks, you will need to paint them completely, one of each color.*

Go to a quiet place, and build a cornmeal circle (page 37). Smudge and step in from the East in honor of your spirit. Remember that when you step into this circle in the Ceremony of Impeccability, that Impeccability is from the spirit out. It is spiritual energy, spiritual thought. Thought obtained from Impeccability brings forth Confidence. When you think with Impeccability, you have Confidence to move forward into Balance, to be Creative, to Grow, to be of Truth, to have Wisdom. And standing there in Impeccability will be the Will of Great Spirit as you see it.

Remember that humans each have their own opinion of the Will of Great Spirit. But Impeccability is. It is perfect. It is clear; it is pure; it is correct. It never harms another or brings injustice or indignity. It isn't selfish; it isn't rude. It isn't prideful. It isn't slanderous or angry. It doesn't condemn. It is straightforward, strong, and steadfast. It is balanced, equal, and fair. It isn't an opinion. It creates; it opens; it expands. Knowing that is the first understanding of the Ceremony of Impeccability.

1. **A circle of candles (or sticks).**
   Sit down inside the circle, and in front of you, draw a circle. Put the burgundy candle, or the burgundy stick, in front of you. To the left, place the red, the orange, then the yellow, then green, blue and purple, and return to the burgundy. You will have made a

circle of candles, or you will have placed a circle of sticks by inserting each stick into the ground.

2. The negatives.

Now I would like you to think of all of the negatives in your life. Do that as you light the candles. First, light the Impeccable candle, thinking of the worst thing that has ever happened to you. List this in your spirit journal.

Then move to the purple candle. Think of the worst insult to you, and light the purple candle with the thought of that insult, or maybe of many insults. List them.

Then move to the blue, thinking of the worst lies that you have known in your life, that have affected you, lies that have been told about you. List them.

Then move to the green, thinking of the worst limits that have been placed on you, how you have limited yourself, how others have limited you. List them.

Moving to the yellow, think of the worst disappointments. List these disappointments.

Move to the orange, thinking of the time you that you have been most misunderstood, and list that.

Move on to the red. Think of the worst loss. The thing that you have lost, that you miss the most, and anguish over. List that loss.

3. The letting go.

Return to burgundy now, and look at the circle again, in a clockwise motion. Start at the burgundy and work your way around, looking at each color. See those things that you have listed disappearing from your mind—disappearing from your life—even though they have passed through your heart as an arrow. Circle them in your mind's eye, looking at each one of those colors, and let go of them. Do this four times, looking at the colors, letting go of those things.

How will you let go? When will you let go? What do you let go of? Looking at the things that other people have done to you, recognize that you have *allowed* those things to affect you. As you look at the clockwise motion of life, as you look at the negatives, as you call them, in your life, or the evils or the bad, your life may seem so extended that it appears to be the world. Maybe you live outside of your life, because you're in fear of everything around you. Perhaps you're worrying constantly about others, and these negatives are stifling your flow forward, keeping you from moving on and having what you want. Look for the anger: who you are mad at, who you have been mad at. What have they done to you? Look at the childishness of it, in your quietness, in these moments. Look at the losses that you have experienced because of your resentments. Make a decision now about where you are going to go, what you are going to do tomorrow.

In your spirit journal, write down the effects of your letting go. Sketch out in your mind simple words.

Example: Good relationships, good roads, children, wellness, long life, openness, owning land and animals.

4. The positives.
Now, starting with the burgundy candle, think of freedom of Will. Move to the red candle. What is the medicine that you deal with in this color? What is the medicine that you walk forward with? It is Confidence. It is having the lesson of Patience in order. So it is Confidence and Patience. Blow out that candle, knowing that you take control of the negative with the positive.

List the actions that make you strong, things that give you purpose. Write a list of strengths that are your Confidence.

List the things that bring about Patience, acts of calmness, quietness, and stillness.

Move to the next candle, the orange one. Think of the things that balance you, and list them. These are the things that unify you. Blow out that candle knowing that you have your life in Balance, that you have Unity.

Move to the yellow candle. List the things that show your creativity, that show you are and can be creative, that you have the lesson of Original. Blow out the yellow candle.

Move to the green. Think of the things that make you grow. List the things that show your growth, the lesson of Faith, the actions of moving forward and having it. Blow out the green candle.

Move to the blue and list your truths, things that are true for you, the lesson of Sincere, knowing what is Sincere for you. Blow out the blue candle.

Move to the purple, listing the things that make you wise, that are your Wisdom, the lesson of Reason, of reasons for you. Blow out the purple candle.

Now move back to the burgundy, and before you put out the

flame, list your Will and Flow. List how you hear spirit, how you see spirit, the types of things that show Great Spirit to you. This is the way to see the Will of Great Spirit. Understand, before you put out the burgundy candle, that you are Absolute. If you wish to harbor anger and hate, then it is your Impeccable way of destruction. Be proud of that and stand in that hate and die for that hate. But look at the true Will of Great Spirit, the Will to love, the Will to be loved, the Will to forgive, the Will to be forgiven. Most of all, the Will to forget and forgive—and let go. Will is not tolerating, not accepting, but forgetting, moving on to the next thing. As you blow out that candle, where are you moving? Where are you going? What are you doing? Will it be the same old habits? Is that your Will? Or is the Will of Great Spirit at hand for you?

If you are using the sticks, when you go around in the negative way (Step 2), think of the negatives as you touch each stick on the top, with the same thoughts that you would use with the candles. Then, when you go clockwise (Step 3), remove each stick from the ground and break it, setting free your Confidence and Balance, your Creativity, your Growth, your Truth, your Wisdom, your Will.

Understand that, from the day this ceremony takes place, you cannot step backwards again. Make yourself a note in your journal.

Example: "I don't do that. I will never do that again. It is not my way to do those things. It is not mine to do that."

From this day on, you will walk away from those things.

When you are done with the ceremony, remove everything, and close the circle in a counter-clockwise manner, picking up each object as you pass.

Totem Rocks

Tools: *Rocks of any size; small rocks for carrying—things for drawing and painting on the rocks such as paint and markers; sage or sweet grass, cornmeal.*

Choose your totem rocks, and put them in a pile in front of you. Sit quietly with the rocks. Breathe in and out very carefully. Reach in front of you and pick up a rock. Hold it in your right hand. Turn your left-hand palm up. Breathe in the energy of the rock. From the rock will come the knowing, through your left hand and in through your mind. Let your eyes close, and you'll begin to see in front of you the spirit of the rock. It will take on a color; it will take on a form. You will see the form of that rock. You will see the animal of that rock. You will recognize the shape—is it a four-legged, a winged one, a hopper, a slithery one, a crawly? You will notice the colors.

Come back with those thoughts, and record them in your spirit journal. Sketch what you have seen. This drawing can be primitive or stick figures or very advanced, artistic, and elaborate. Then take a pencil and sketch what you have seen onto the rock. Then paint it on the rock. Put a circle of color around the border of the drawing. The color should be the totem color of the animal, the color that you know the spirit of the animal to be from your vision. Then look at the colors and see the power of this animal. Is it red? Is it orange? Is it yellow? Green? Blue? Is it purple? Is it burgundy? Is it black or white—silver or gold? The color and animal become a guide in your life to help you with your direction of a good life.

It is always a good thing to look up synonyms of words and to look up synonyms of the synonyms. Look up definitions in the dictionary and thesaurus. Get a clear understanding of what power this animal has brought you. Know that this totem is a part of you. It is you, brought forth in a totem rock. The animal will guide you, giving you strength and power.

When you have finished painting the rocks, they are yours to carry. You can have totem animals, totem spirits, totem colors for your four directions. You can find a totem rock for each color in your medicine wheel to guide you in your spirit. Your totem animal may change. You can look and see each day if it is the same. If not, find a new totem for yourself. Make a new rock; carry the rock. When you are done with the rock, you can gift it to another and tell the story of the totem rock. Or you can give the rock back to the earth, and let it go. You do that by placing the rock on the earth and seeing your totem go away.

Totem Rock

The Process of the Lesson of Worth

Tools: *Cornmeal; sage or sweet grass; sacred tools of your choice; spirit journal and pen.*

Build a cornmeal circle (page 37), smudge, and enter the circle with your spirit journal and pen.

1. **Spirit self.**

   Think about all the things you know about your spirit. Sit very still, cross-legged, with your palms up, and breathe in through your nose and out through your mouth four times. Close your eyes and continue breathing. Before you, you will see darkness. That darkness will become a light blue. In that blue, you will begin to see a spirit. Pay attention to what that spirit looks like. Walk around it; examine it carefully. It will stand there as if it's a model, and show itself to you. It will turn around; it will fly if it can; it will hop and run if it can. It will show you itself, its color, what it looks like in the animal world, what it looks like in the plant world. What it looks like in the human world is you.

   This is your spirit self. Remember it, bring it back, and record it in your spirit journal. It is important to have a relationship with your spirit self, to accept what your spirit is, what it is capable of doing. You will know these things by interpreting what you have seen.

2. **Acceptance.**

   We must all accept in our lives, the wrongs and the rights, the lies and the truths. We must sit with the good and the bad and sort through them. Sometimes it seems as if all of us two-leggeds have lost our ability to accept each others' ways. Sometimes we go beyond what is necessary to control and condemn others' lives.

   To achieve Worth, we must have acceptance of the self—the spirit self and the physical self.

   Make a list of everything that you are physically.

   Example: Teacher, visionary, shaman, woman, wife, sister, aunt.

   Make a list of the essence of your spirit self.

   Example: Blue, burgundy, white, wolf.

Putting your two lists together, write a paragraph about yourself, accepting yourself for what you are. As you do it, start by looking for the first, second, and third colors. Also write about the animals, plants, and rocks that you see.

Example: Clan color—burgundy. Band—blue. Totem animal—the wolf. Its physical color—white. The spirit medicine of wolf is a spirit teacher, one of strength. This life is one of Impeccable Truth, and walks with spirit.

3. Memories.

There are two kinds of memories—physical memories and spiritual memories. Physical memories are made up of teachings. They happen at times when you are contained, instructed, controlled, or guided.

Example: When you are structured to believe a doctrine and given no freedom to change that structure (medical procedures, legal procedures, governmental, military, or religious procedures), and when you're involved in arguments, grief and death, these are controlled physical memories. When you are involved in sports, driving, flying, cooking, mathematics, these are contained physical memories. When you are involved in music, art, drama, some sports like golf and archery, all the martial arts, these are instructed physical memories. When you meet a loved one for the first time, have a great time, experience joy—it is a guided physical memory.

All physical memories are energy.

To understand memory is to look at your past life. Your physical form may never have lived before, but your spirit is energy. Energy is spirit. Your spirit has been eternal and always will be eternal. So, what are the memories of your spirit? What constitutes who you are, as you stand in your fullness?

Spiritual memories make up a very strong part of who you are and what your purpose is on this earth. They are involved with color, harmonics, feelings, essence, clarity.

Example: Times when you are a dream state—night dreams, daydreams, visions, and guided journeys, are memories of colors. When you are sound, being music, involved with present sound (such as rain, wind blowing, traffic, people talking) are mem-

143

ories of harmonics. Being open, receiving knowledge, prayer, understanding visions, understanding language, to love, are memories connected with feelings. When smells are involved, all sounds, all sightings and sights, taste and touch, and also color (again), you are involved with essence. Understanding, intelligence, prayer as communication, motivation, spirituality, expression have to do with clarity.

All spiritual memories are constant.

Sit in a quiet place within your circle, breathe and relax. Take four deep breaths in through your nose and out through your mouth, and walk into a realm of memory.

Write down the memories of your physical life—where you went to school, who your friends were, the kind of people you associated with, the kinds of places you went. Why were you called to where you were called? Often, in our lives, we are called to a place where we entered or exited previously.

Example: If you have a fascination with trains, you might have entered or exited the realm of physicality through an experience of a train. Perhaps that is where your energy was during a train accident, and that is where you exited the world once before.

It's important to understand your memories and to ask yourself why you are intensely drawn to something. You may be drawn to things because you have a broken heart, because something was taken from you. It may have been wrongfully altered, and you were not able to go on through the flow that you expected.

Example: Memories of Christmas that haunt you—candies, cookies, and smells; things that, when you get close to them, leave you empty, alone, and scared. You may have been in an extremely ugly or brutal whirl or argument through which the atmosphere of the holiday was broken down. If the ceremony was disrupted by hate and dissension, you might feel a haunting that would call you to it, and you would need to work through your memory and let go of these things.

Take four deep breaths again, in through your nose and out through your mouth, and relax. You are now going to walk to a realm of spiritual memories. Let them just come to you, and write them down—memories of spirit colors, of spirit places, of surroundings where you have been a part of the energy forever. List them.

This ceremony needs to be completed in order to allow your spirit to go on and experience what your physical life gives it as a memory.

4. Joy.

Joy is a combination of ability, understanding, knowing, dreams, visions, support, and happiness. The spiritual side of joy allows the spirit to flow and be seen as the fullness of life. Our joy of spirit is seen and felt through music, art, nature, actions of drama, and interaction of culture. Color and sounds bring forth joy from the spirit. Also the spirit is rich and full from the knowing of spiritual truth, as in the wind's voice, the song of the rain, the face of the snow, and the riches of fire. Each person has the physical part of joy, which is chemical and very precious. But chemicals must be balanced. The physical part of the brain is very fragile and easy to disturb. When your dreams are broken, your understanding squashed, your ability denied, or your knowing is deferred, severe trauma may take place. The chemicals in the body react and may produce extreme anger and rage. Stress, drugs, and chemical abuse will alter joy, which is dangerous because joy perpetuates Worth.

Look at the things that are your abilities. Write them down. Write your understanding, your Knowing—knowing what you can do, knowing what you must do in order to do what you want. Write down your dreams. Formulating dreams, carrying the dreams out, having the dreams come true, is one way to truly experience joy. Having the ability to carry out a dream means organizing it—making the list that we call a 1–25. Put things in front of you that allow you to succeed. Put a path before you that gives you an understanding that Confidence is your medicine, that Balance is your medicine, that, yes, there is good and bad in life, but if you dwell on the bad, you will become the bad. It is within joy that we erase the knowledge of anger, that we erase the knowledge of bitterness, of sadness and sorrow. Joy is a burst of energy that propels us to succeed.

· 10 ·

CROSSOVER

I take a deep breath. I put on my black hat. My assistant holds my medicine coat while I put it on. I hear the tinkling of the bells and the rumble of the rattles. The spirit of the medicine embraces me. I step outside the lodge and walk onto the grounds. The preparation for this ceremony has taken place; the yard is fresh and green; the prayer ties are blowing softly in the breeze; the fires are lit, and the smoke spirals into the air.

All of the teachings of the weeks gone by are now bundles. These bundles have been wrapped in colors—bundles of red, bundles of yellow, bundles of orange, bundles of purple, bundles of burgundy, bundles of blue, and bundles of green. They have been laid down, one after another, to bring forth a Rainbow Bridge for the students to cross over. Poles stand by the bridge of bundles, with paper and soft cloth tied on them, whispering in the breeze. These represent the spirit—each student's spirit.

The ceremony is going to take place in the lives of those who have walked in these studies known as Rainbow Medicine, in the lives of those students who have quested for their whole self. It is a time of celebration. They have sat in sacred ceremonies and looked themselves in the face; they have gotten to know their spirit better. They have let go of childhood pains and worked on memory.

I look around the ceremonial grounds. I see the kitchen area, with steam coming from the cookers. The tables are set to greet the food.

The teaching area has become a sacred site now, where these students will cross the bridge, the sacred representation of Crossover. They are crossing over from not knowing the Truth of Great Spirit, Grandmother/Grandfather; from not having their beliefs in order. They are crossing over from being told what to do, to choosing to do it their own way. I represent both worlds—the white, the Caucasian, and the Native American; many races of people come to the medicine circle. I think that all people were meant to come together in a circle.

What I see when I look at the medicine wheel is the way of the eagle. I see the eagle soar over our heads and circle, giving out its whistle. I see the way of the coyote, the lessons of life, the lessons of Patience and Unity, of Original, the lessons of Faith and Sincere, Reason, and Worth. I think when these people came in the gate, they came as lost two-leggeds who had been lied to and deceived. I think they walked through the sacredness of red, through purple into burgundy in their hearts. I think their sacred hearts have been opened. This day I look at their lodge poles and see what they feel about their existence.

There is great anticipation among the staff as they wait for these two-leggeds to arrive. On their wrists they wear the colored bands that represent the medicine they have listened to. Is Patience a lesson or a teaching now? Has Worth become a lesson or a teaching? The celebration of Crossover is the Ceremony of the Sacred Self. It is a time when their spirit names are whispered. I listen to the spiraling whistle, the call of the eagle. I think of the bear, the medicine that is deep inside. Do they understand the blending of two worlds? Do they understand the respect and magic in nature? The sacred circle of life? I see the wolf standing in the distance, its eyes looking straight at me. As I stand in the sacred site waiting for the students to arrive with their guests to witness their ceremony, the wolf in me is the path leader, the guide, the parent, the protector.

I breathe in and out, and watch the smoke spiral in front of me. Within it I see the Rainbow Dragon, the keeper of the fire, the one who tends the logs, the one who is the fire. To the right is the Black Horse, who waits—the judge of all judges, the exquisite, Impeccable one that we know as death. On the left I see the *Chanupa*, the sacred pipe, and with it the White Buffalo Woman, the carrier. It is between life and death that we live a physical existence—from prayer to the end of the cycle, the cutting away, the readying, the dropping of the robe. I close my eyes and open them to reality.

The students gather at the drum in ceremony, and they drum together. They drum in the solemnness of Crossover. The ceremony goes on, the eating, talking, and celebrating. The students are proud. They stand with their spirit names, whispered in the wind. They walk with Soft Wind, Tree Song, Lightning Moon Dog, White Arrow, Eagle Wolf, Black Wolf. River Horse stands there. Blue Bird. Many students, many Crossover ceremonies spiral through my mind. I have seen many for I am a giver of life.

I take a deep breath in and let it out. Before me in the field I see a black and white horse. It is the spirit horse that waits to carry our spirit across the Rainbow Bridge. As the students cross the Rainbow Bridge in the physical reality, they are holding themselves accountable to their faith and belief. They are making a statement that they believe their spirit will sing to them, and they will follow their spiritual path of Truth eternally. Each student is invited to dance the sacred path, to go on within the study of the shields, to explore the feeling road that lies ahead of us, the path of wholeness.

The smoke rises as the prayer ties are placed in the fire pit and burned. The smoke carries the prayers to Great Spirit, Grandmother/Grandfather. Many legends live within these fences. The most sacred of all beliefs breathes in and out. The wind spirits sing; sunlight embraces us. The soft, small drops of rain wash away, and the song of the frog comes on.

The doors of the lodge are opened. The invitation to dance the Sacred Dance is given. What lies ahead of us are the emotions, the second section of our Medicine Wheel. I explain to the students that we will once again light the candles in the second phase of our existence, the emotion phase. For within the spiritual phase, we have stood, and we have learned. We have the medicines of Confidence, Balance, Creativity, Growth, Truth, Wisdom, and Impeccability. We leave with the lessons from Worth to Patience. They can become teachings of Unity. They can be teachings of Patience. They can be held in totality and lived. When that happens, you dance the sacred beats.

Come with me now. Follow me to the Sacred Dance. Seven step forth, and seven go on with me—to lessons of Clarity and Discipline, Fact and Sense. To medicines of Beauty and Power, Greatness and Strength. It is ours, as we step forth . . .

I hear the soft sound of the flute calling us back.

Ceremony of the Self

The ceremony of the self is to be done alone, in a quiet place, where you cannot be disturbed, outside where you can feel the wind and be in touch with all. When you go to this place, make sure you will be alone for an hour or more. Choose a quiet spot alongside the river, or at the ocean, in a park, in the woods, or in the quiet of your own back yard.

With your spirit journal and pen, put yourself in a position to record the ceremony of your sacred self.

1. Your breath.

Sit quietly and breathe four breaths in and out. While you are breathing, ask yourself, "What is the purpose in breath?" Then answer the question, "Why do you breathe?" Breathe in and out very slowly and very evenly. Find the purpose of your breath—what your breath is to you—and write it down in your spirit journal.

Example: My breathing is my support system. It is my next step in life. My breath is Confidence to me. It is my connection to physical existence, and as I breathe in and out, I am alive.

2. Your body.

Look at your hands. Look at your feet. Think of your body in a mirror, your whole self. What color is your hair? What color are your eyes? What is your physical self? What is the purpose in having a body? In your spirit journal, answer the questions to yourself.

Example: My body allows me to have a Balance between spirit and physical. It gives me the opportunity to feel, to be tangible, to experience life and death.

3. Your feelings.

Let your eyes close softly. Before you, you'll begin to see your feelings taking form. Look at what color they are, or what animal they represent themselves as, how they feel to you. Are you at peace? Are you enraged? Are you delicate? Are you excited? Relax, and listen to the wind around you. Open your eyes and look around. Think about what your feelings are to you. How do they matter to you? Who is in charge of your feelings? What are your feelings to you? Record this in your spirit journal.

Example: My feelings are doorways. They are opportunities to go beyond. Yesterday I was that, and today I am this. Tomorrow I will be that. I can travel the road of many lives in my mind through reading books and watching movies. I can open doors for others. I can give myself the opportunity to think anything I wish, for my feelings are my Creativity.

4. What is you.

Take a deep breath in, and hold it as long as you can; then let it go. As you do, think of a place that is you.

Take a deep breath in, and hold it as long as you can; then let it go. Think of a color that is you.

Take a deep breath in, and hold it as long as you can. Think of anything that is you. Feel anything. See it for what it is.

Take a deep breath in and hold it. Let it go and know, and see, and feel, and have your sacred self.

Write about your sacred self in your spirit journal. You get it from the place, from the color, from anything and everything. Put down in your spirit journal what your sacred self is.

> *Example:* The lofty mountain is covered with white snow. Snow spiraling around. A crystal clear blue sky, a blue that is deep and boundless. A burgundy sunset. A wolf. A woman. A teacher. A shaman. Sacred Medicine of the Great What Is. Messenger of God. My sacred self.

Record these feelings and the essence of your sacred self in your spirit journal. When you are done, breathe in what you are and be grateful for what you are. Go forward in the sacredness of your Confidence, to the Impeccability of the Sacred Self.

Celebration Spirit Pole

Tools: *A pole 5 to 7 feet (1.5 to 2m) tall; colored thread; colored cloth; objects that represent celebration to you; sage and sweet grass*

A celebration spirit pole is put together out of a celebration of your sacred self. This pole is very special. To find the right one, go for a walk by the beach or in the woods, or anywhere where you can find a long pole or stick. It should be long enough so that you can bury the base in the ground in your yard. If you live in an apartment, you would place it by your front door. In any case, tie things onto the pole to celebrate your spirit self, to celebrate the sacred self of the spirit.

Place things on this pole that are you.

> *Example:* I'll tie a sun, a moon, and seven colored stars on mine. There will be wolf fur. There will be things that come from the ocean that represent my depth, things that come from pine trees which represent my life. I will wrap it in colors: first white, then soft blue, then

strong blue, then red, orange, yellow, green, blue, purple, and bur-
gundy, then black, then soft blue, then white. I'll tie strands of stars
that twinkle and glitter, that reflect life everlasting. I'll put long
streamers of cloth on it that can sway in the breeze, that represent
my freedom. I'll hang bells on it.

When you have put together your celebration spirit pole, it will need a place that is special in your yard. Put it where you can see it every day, where you can celebrate your life, where you can go to it and place cornmeal and tobacco, where you can walk past it every day and be grateful. Put it out where people can see it and ask you what it is. And you can tell them it is a celebration spirit pole, where you celebrate your life, and that you walk in contemporary Native American teachings that *allow you* to celebrate your life.

Place it in the ground, and circle it four times in honor of the four directions. Raise your hands to Great Spirit, and give thanks for your joy, which shows on this pole. Around the base of it you can plant flowers to represent the life that you have. You can plant anything that you wish that represents life. Then, around that, put a circle of rocks that closes in the pole, a sacred circle of rock. This represents the care that you bring to your sacred life.

You can add to your celebration spirit pole any time you wish. I add fresh flowers for special events and celebrations: at deaths, at births, and at other times I wish to connect with my sacred self and be thankful for what I have in life.

The Process of Wholeness

The process of wholeness is achieved by having a celebration, by putting together a representation of yourself.

Example: Cooking a meal that represents your Creativity. Reading aloud from your favorite book a passage that is strong, that brings you presence of mind, and puts you forth on a steady path. Listening to music that is your spirit singing, unbound. Sitting quietly in the yard, watching birds fly, representing the freedom of your spirit.

The process of your wholeness is made of seven steps—one for Confidence, one for Balance, one for Creativity, one for Growth, one for Truth, one for Wisdom, and one for Impeccability. Put together an evening, a day, an afternoon or even an hour of time that is the process of your wholeness, something that you can share with other people. Invite at least one other person to experience the process of wholeness with you.

> **Example:** *The person comes to your house. You sit outside and watch the birds fly. You come inside, where there is music that represents you, your inner core. You listen to the sounds of the music while you share a meal. Afterwards, you retire in front of the fireplace for quiet reading, where you share your sacred self.*

Your process of wholeness is a celebration and a ceremony of your sacred self to be done as you see fit. It is a special time for you to have a Crossover, to show that you are walking the Rainbow Path.

Aho.

For more information, contact
Wolf Moondance at P.O. Box 788,
Richland, Washington 99352

MEDICINE INTERPRETATIONS

The following interpretations, written from a contemporary standpoint, have been brought to me through years of experience in the two legged and spirit worlds. I have presented them to help you understand the medicines and lessons.

Medicine Words

Red—Confidence. Confidence is the connection with pure energy, and the ability to live your physical life in memory and example of Great Spirit, which is Clarity. It is being accountable to the memory of spirit and bringing purity of spirit to action in a physical way—in human existence. It is believing that you can.

Orange—Balance. The point of reality that owns all, this is the coming together of spirit and physical. It is the point that gives breath the opportunity to be. Balance is acceptance of "evil" and "good" and coming to the point of "all is a good thing."

Yellow—Creativity. This awe-inspiring movement is perpetual motion, bringing forth the opportunity to design. It is thought precipitating matter—principle, opportunity, thought, movement, gain, material, experience, spirituality. Physicality is Creativity.

Green—Growth. Experience and the ability to respond to Creativity. The pleasure of physicality. Growth is a doorway, an opportunity in which pain can be experienced. It is the ability to take pain and turn it into gain. Growth is the mark of understanding self.

Blue—Truth. Vastness, depth, and sincerity—a level of compatibility that intertwines. A platform. A constant. An Is. The Truth births all Truth.

155

The Truth, the Great What Is. The ability to stand in point of Balance and be filled with Creativity. Truth resonates; it sings; it births, and it lives.

Purple—Wisdom. Collected memory of Truth that is brought about from Growth, which is the Song of Creativity. Wisdom is the opportunity of realizing experience, which allows you to stand in two worlds—where you were and where you are. It is the rectifying balance point that gives you the opportunity to step in and step out at the same time. It is success and failure for it brings about experience. It is a cloak; it is a dagger. It is a snare; it is the sky.

Burgundy—Impeccability. It is darkest before the dawn. Impeccability is constant; it is consistent. It was and always will be. Perfection of constant, the foreverness of consistent. It is the quiet before the storm. Within Impeccability is sanity, for it is conditional that there is no unconditional to constant. Impeccability is giving it your all, 100 percent of the time—being able to reach for the stars, daring to dream, and standing upon the dream with exquisite Faith. It is the resonance and perpetual motion of Creativity and Truth. It is the Purity of Clarity, it is the heart and mind of Great Spirit. Eternal.

Lesson Words

Red—Patience. When Patience is a lesson, it is the opponent. It is the quest; it is the challenge; it is the opportunity. Calm, still, and quiet!

Orange—Unity. When it is a lesson, it is a challenge to be one with it. It is a striving to become. It is a longing for peace. When it is a teaching— when it has been learned—it is a settling, being at peace with, bringing about clarity. It resonates harmony and tranquility. A good neighbor. A good friend. A good loved one. A circle with a point of all.

Yellow—Original. When it is a lesson, it is a striving to become. It is the push, it is the standing up, it is the striving to conquer. It is unique. Only when it becomes a teaching—when it is learned—is it united. It is a joining that brings about the Great What Is. Original is total. It is flow at peace.

Green—Faith. As a lesson, Faith is a challenge. It is illusive and hard; it is cold and straightforward. When it is learned—when it has become a teaching—it is calm and deep. It is settled and full. The ability to understand belief at its fullest—Confidence being stood upon—Faith is.

Blue—Sincere. As a lesson, it is proving. It is to prove oneself in totality— to be the warrior, to be the quester. To seek out. To take it to the limit. When it is learned, it is a teaching; it is humble. It is respectful; it's orderly; it's united; it's steadfast.

Purple—Reason. When Reason is a lesson, it is questioning, a setting out to find, a thirst for answers. When it is a teaching—when it has been learned—it is the answer; it is the solidity, the point, the spirit of action; it is purpose.

Burgundy—Worth. When Worth is a lesson, it is hard. It is empty; it is big; it is vast and ever present. When it is a teaching, it is a shield; it is solidity; it is proof; it is power; it is exquisite. It is Impeccable. It is all.

Acknowledgments

The sound of the drum, the song and the singer, the dance and the dancer. The way of the teacher. It is my heart to dedicate these works to those who walk in those ways. I acknowledge those who hear something and look and see it. Those who see something and know what they saw. Those who never quit because it's the dream that pushes you towards the vision that brings life into its fullness. I acknowledge the one who had a vision, who stood tall enough and strong enough to dare to dream and achieve that vision.

To Geri, Katherine, Sharon and Vickie—you've assisted well. It was my vision and my dream and you believed in me. For those moments that you served, you are formally thanked.

To my family, for their love and support: Betty, Tyler, Neil and Helen. Blood is thicker than water.

To my wolf. Her four feet pound the concrete beside me, the dirt I walk on, the day that we share. To Chimmey—thank you.

To Sheila Anne, for caring and helping once more.

I acknowledge and thank Granny Jo, for her hard work, for her fingers that dance these words to physicality. For her belief and support as a student and Black Hat.

To my half side. My heart is filled with joy for there is never a day that I am abandoned or not good enough, or neglected or forgotten, or not treated with the utmost respect and honor. Unto you I carry our secret name. I hold within myself the center that I draw from. And here again, another work has happened. I give thanks to you for your support. Always. And I will wait on the other side of the bridge. Aho.

Index

160